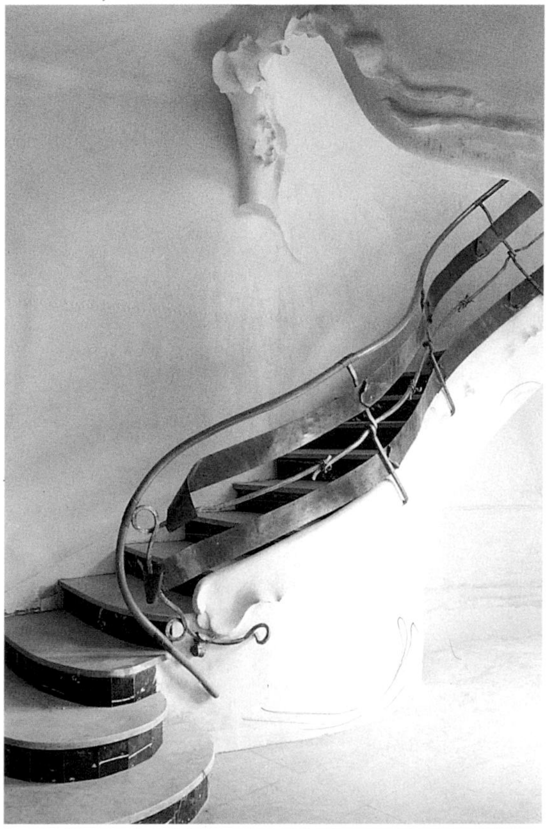

INFLUENTIAL INTERIORS

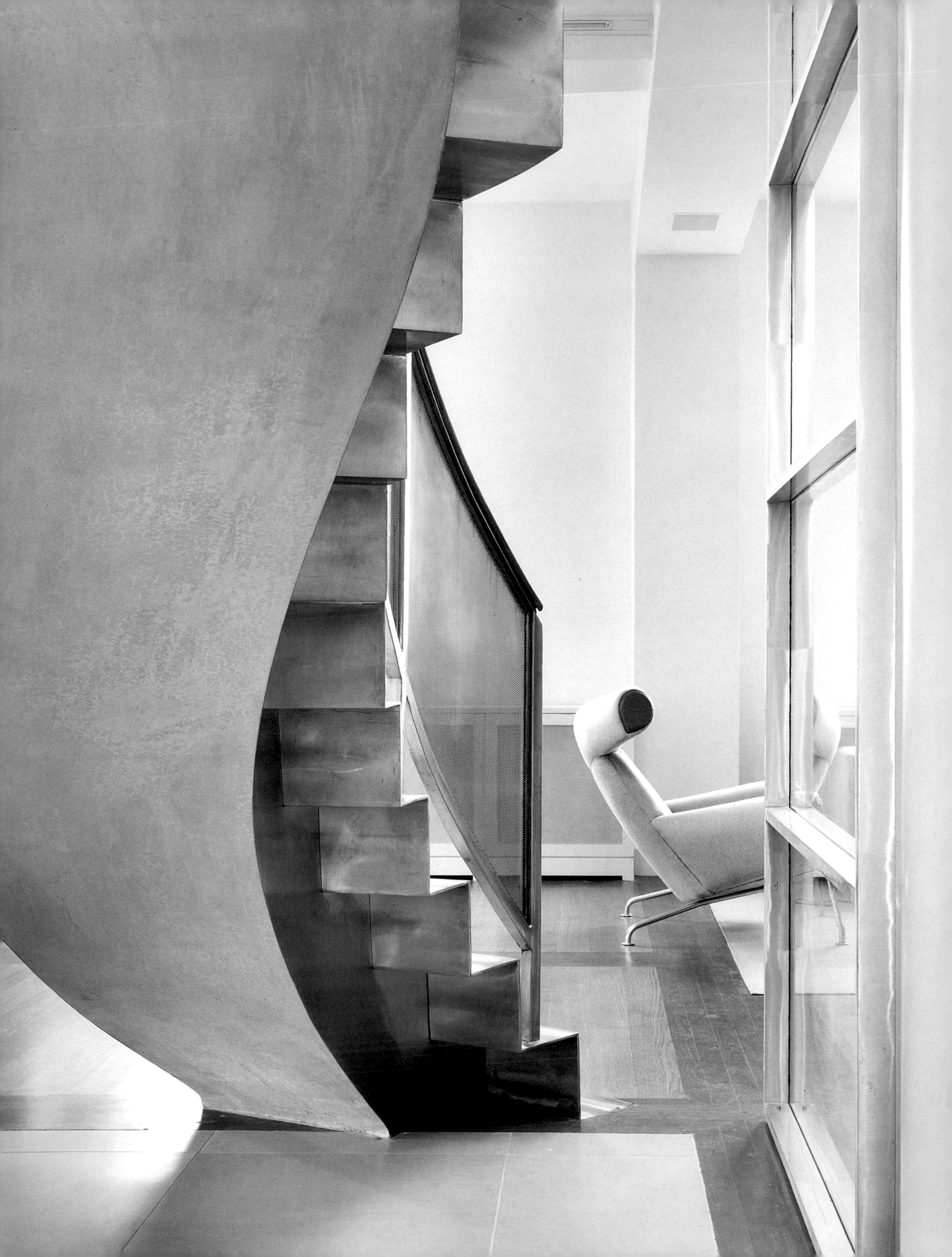

INFLUENTIAL
INTERIORS

SUZANNE TROCME

MITCHELL BEAZLEY

First published in Great Britain in 1999
by Mitchell Beazley,
an imprint of Octopus Publishing Group Ltd
2–4 Heron Quays, London E14 4JP

Executive Editor **Judith More**
Executive Art Editor **Janis Utton**
Project Editor **Julia North**
Editor **Catherine Rubinstein**
Designer **Tony Spalding**
Picture Researcher **Claire Gouldstone**
Production Controller **Karen Farquhar**

A CIP record for this book is available from the British Library.

ISBN 1 84000 101 1

Printed in China by Toppan Printing Co Ltd

Page 1: The staircase of the Torre de la Creu in Barcelona by Josep Maria Jujol, 1913. The double-apartment ground plan consisted of five intersecting cylinders, two of which held the staircases.

Page 2: The curving stainless-steel and concrete staircase leading to the cylindrical gallery in the apartment of Lee Mindel, of Shelton, Mindel & Associates, New York, 1998.

Pages 4/5: A new stone fireplace in a late Victorian house in London, interior-designed by Jenny Armit.

Page 6: Contemporary comfort in Marbella by Alberto Pinto.

CONTENTS

FOREWORD

In approaching this project, I realized from the onset in talking to some of the designers that the only way to compose *Influential Interiors* would be to do as the designers themselves do which, in response to client needs, involves more listening in the beginning than anything else. Then comes the assimilation of information, followed by the interpretation.

It seemed only fitting that the designers covered in this book should have a voice and freedom to explain why they have chosen interior design as their métier, who has provided their main inspiration, and what has continued to encourage and spur them on. In short, their passions and admissions. Many covered are not purely interior designers but have in many respects shaped the way our interiors have evolved: Philippe Starck and Ettore Sottsass are two who would not normally use the label "interior designer" to describe their contributions to our environment, but contribute nonetheless. Some people included talked about the past, others discussed where they see the future. Most were expressive, animated, even prescient, and all were delighted to be part of the project. It is a pity that some, like David Hicks, who seemed to so enjoy the relaxed nature of the interviews, are not here to witness the publication of the book, which is intended to be a frank and informative guide to some of the key taste-makers of our century, with a defined accent on domestic interior design.

Influential Interiors is not intended to be encyclopaedic: it is a selective study of our interior spaces, past and present, by some of the most visionary creators. It concentrates on the history of interior design as a profession and on the development of ideas – whether derived from official movements with strong manifestos or simply stemming from interesting but significant moments of inspiration. The profession of interior design has existed only for the last hundred years – here explored under six visual "umbrellas" or chapter headings. Highlighting seminal moments in 20th-century interior design history, the book seeks to address much of the crossover occurring throughout the creative industries and the relationships between architecture, art, fashions and the interior. Moreover, it is a celebration of the very personal work that the best in the field undertake today.

Having had the opportunity to meet and talk at length with the influential designers, their friends and their families, and having found answers to many of my own questions about the provenance of some of the room designs and objects we see around us, I have come to wholeheartedly believe in the thought expressed by the publisher Malcolm Forbes (1919-90) who said, quite plainly, "Contrary to the cliché, genuinely nice guys often finish first or very near it."

Suzanne Trocmé, 1999

OPULENT

Lavish interiors have been popular among the nobility of Europe for several centuries. A succession of richly opulent styles, such as Baroque, Rococo and, later, the Beaux-Arts, have evolved and flourished, often originating in France before spreading across the rest of Europe and America. These decorative styles are on the whole far more subtle than they may seem: it takes an experienced designer, inspired yet restrained, to draw together the elements of such finery to create interiors with some degree of permanence and lasting impact.

Above: Paris-based decorator Alberto Pinto has restored and redesigned this salon in the spirit of Louis XVI. The Louis XIV doors of the *grand salon* give onto the *petit salon*, which is painted in delicate blue tones. The *guéridon* in bronze is by Thomire and the sculpture is signed Carrier Belleuse.

Previous pages: Alberto Pinto's *grand salon* in Paris reinterprets *Empire* style, particularly Parisian *Empire*, as evident in the doors. Venetian stucco walls support two English paintings; German and Austrian furniture is grouped on a large Aubusson rug. The cushions or pillows are antique tapestry, some of them pearl-embroidered in Louis XIV fashion.

In the Middle Ages, after the collapse of the Roman Empire, when the amenities of domestic life so developed by the Romans (such as central heating) were lost to Europe, interior decoration in the contemporary sense can hardly be said to have existed at all. In those war-stricken times, the only question about a home was how to defend it.

The history of interior decoration is patchy for the next few centuries. The Crusades must have introduced many Europeans to Oriental carpets, but the record is enigmatic. However, the observant Venetian traveller Marco Polo wrote of the beauty of Turkish Anatolian rugs, and noted that courtiers in China donned white leather slippers before stepping on the elaborate silk carpets.

By the later Middle Ages, the great houses of France were decorated with tapestries, which served the dual purpose of providing visual interest and keeping out at least some of the drafts. They also signified wealth and status, and were handed down in families from generation to generation and moved from castle to castle. The Dukes of Burgundy even hung them in their tents while on campaign.

Meanwhile the Italians were painting their palace and villa walls with images in which fantasy was given free rein. Around the 14th century, the Renaissance inspired new interest in classical tradition. Families like the Medici, Este and Farnese celebrated their glory in terms of Greek and Latin mythology and created murals recording the love affairs of their princes, who must have thought themselves comparable with Aeneas and Jupiter.

The French were soon influenced by Italian style – by Raphael's wall-paintings in the Vatican, Giorgio Vasari's historical paintings in Florence and Giulio Romano's frescoes in Mantua. Tapestries of knights and their ladies were exiled from French walls and replaced by painted scenes from the *Iliad* or the *Aeneid* and episodes from the love life of Jupiter. Italian painters, stucco artists, founders and engravers of bronze, jewellers, architects and garden designers were invited to Fontainebleau, in northern France, where they trained French artists and craftsmen. During the reigns of François I and his son, Henri II (which together spanned the years 1515–59), France was introduced to a completely new style of decoration by Italian artists.

It could be said that modern decoration began in the chateaux of Fontainebleau and Oiron (the latter decorated in 1546–9, although its ceilings were finished in the 17th century), since these were the first interiors created as the affluent became aware of alternative styles and methods of decoration and began to make aesthetic choices about their surroundings. Of course, only the extremely rich could indulge in such expressions of wealth, but the ensuing centuries provide numerous illustrations of lavish and luxurious interiors commissioned by kings, princes and noblemen.

Baroque & Rococo

The Italian Renaissance interior was characterized by the use of classical architectural features such as pillars, entablatures and heavy mouldings, and a wealth of other ornament inspired by classical sources. Reclining *amorini* (cupids), floral garlands, grotesque and lion masks, scrollwork and cornucopia are among the most familiar.

Baroque, which originated in Rome in the late 16th century as an architectural development of late Renaissance style, affected decoration of interiors across Europe in the 17th and early 18th centuries. Use of painted panelling, marble and plasterwork continued, and Renaissance motifs were incorporated, but execution and arrangement were heavier, richer, bolder and more theatrical than the Renaissance image.

The Baroque style was borrowed by many European countries and adapted to national tastes, reaching its apex in the second half of the 17th century in France. French Baroque can be roughly divided into three stages: first the style of Louis XIII (reigned 1610–43), then that of Louis XIV (reigned 1643–1715), and finally the period of transition into the Rococo style, which quickly spread through the courts of Europe, from Russia to Spain, from England to Italy. Rococo (also known as *Régence*, although the style did not actually come into being during the French Regency of 1715–23, but in about 1690) distilled the nectar from Baroque, emphasizing its sweetest elements. It was the most feminine of the French periods (*Empire*, the style of the early 19th century, was the most masculine). Rococo architects, designers, craftsmen and artists together created a light, delicate impression, lively and full of movement and colour. Shell motifs and leaf scrolls appeared, in asymmetric yet well-balanced form, painted, then gilded or silvered. Superb examples of rooms decorated in this style are found at Chantilly in France and the Amalienburg in Bavaria.

The boom in opulent decoration during the Baroque period cannot be attributed to individual personalities or tastes of kings alone. French expansion in Asia and America, and growth in national wealth, enriched the aristocracy, leading to the building of the palace of Versailles and the magnificent Galerie d'Apollon at the Louvre in Paris. Prosperity was reflected in the grandeur of architecture and decoration: the *grand salon* came into being, staircases became more stately, and the first unified decorative scheme was executed.

19th-century styles

A century and a revolution later, in 1801, the French nobility returned to Paris at Napoleon's invitation, and took up residence again in their great 18th-century houses in the Faubourg St Honoré, the Chaussée d'Antin and the Place de la Concorde.

Below: The engaging feature of this splendid office – in a private home by Alberto Pinto – is its refinement, accented by the *boiserie*, particularly the relief created by the colour mix; the *boiserie* is painted in four tones of gold and silver. The Boulle desk is from the Louis XIV period, as is the carpet.

Above: French decorator Jacques Garcia's interest in foreign parts inspired this colourful corridor in a neo-Gothic apartment in Paris, which has a design taken from a colonnade from Persia applied onto a background of red cloth.

The wealthy nobles, grateful to be alive after the revolution, wasted little time in ridding their residences of pre-revolutionary Rococo excesses and adopting their Emperor's taste for rectilinear mahogany furniture, classical symbols celebrating honour and patriotism, and geometrically laid-out rooms. This rich neoclassical style was later known as *Empire* or French Empire. The cost involved in revamping the vast residences was massive, but the expenditure demonstrated to the world that not all wealth was lost in the revolution of 1789 and France still had an aristocracy (if with reduced privileges), as well as showing Napoleon that, at least on the surface, the aristocracy accepted him. The impressive two-storied Napoleonic *grands salons*, where masked balls and dances were held, may have been less ornate than their predecessors, but by today's standards were opulent nonetheless.

Britain, meanwhile, was experiencing the influence of its own empire. Travel to foreign lands has played a significant role in the history of the opulent interior, partly because travel in itself is indicative of a lifestyle of pecuniary ease that may allow decorative indulgences, and many travellers enjoy incorporating themes from faraway places in their rooms. At the end of the 18th century there were about 600 maharajas in northwestern India, living in lavish palaces. As British trade with India increased, so did Western interest in Indian culture. This was encouraged by British artists' paintings of Indian scenery and customs, and led to a brief flourishing of Indian-influenced buildings in Britain. In 1803, Sir Charles Cockerell, "an eminent servant of the East India Company," gave an Indian flavour to his new house at Sezincote, in Gloucestershire. The onion domes crowning its roof increased general interest in the Indian style, and the then Prince of Wales adopted the image for his stables at Brighton on the south coast. He was so delighted with the result that he commissioned John Nash to design a major building with an Indian-style exterior – now known as the Royal Pavilion, Brighton.

The Victorian era – taken, stylistically, to commence in 1815, although the British Queen Victoria did not ascend the throne until 1837 – saw the growth of an increasingly better-off middle-class population. Uncertain of their own tastes and too nervous to experiment, the middle classes turned to tried-and-tested styles of previous eras. A profusion of revival styles and decorative reinterpretations was seen in both Britain and North America. Prominent among them was European Renaissance Revival, which remained in vogue until around 1850, when Gothic Revival, inspired by Medieval churches and Elizabethan and Jacobean domestic styles, took precedence.

The Beaux-Arts

At the beginning of the 20th century, the prevalent style for grand interiors was the Beaux-Arts, whose source was the teaching of the *Ecole des Beaux-Arts* in Paris. Inspired by French classical architecture of the 17th and 18th centuries, Beaux-Arts adherents created an atmosphere of grandeur for large hotels, opera-houses, ostentatious homes and department stores, due in part to the use of extravagant lighting. A graduate of the Beaux-Arts school, Jean-Louis Charles Garnier (1825–98), created the foyer of the Paris Opéra, one of the better-known examples. This opera-house, and the Beaux-Arts style in general, influenced the design and decoration of many public buildings around the world. The leading exponent of the Beaux-Arts style in Britain was the firm of Mewes and Davis, responsible for the design of London's Ritz Hotel in 1903–6. However, the influence of the Beaux-Arts was most evident in the United States. Richard Morris Hunt (1827–95) was the first American to study at the Beaux-Arts; returning home in 1855, he designed French Renaissance Revival mansions in New York and Long Island for the millionaires W. K. Vanderbilt and J. J. Astor. Another graduate of the school, Charles Follen McKim, became part of a team responsible for the grand interiors of the Boston Public Library and the Pierpoint Morgan Library in New York. Today, leading American decorators continue to create fine interiors for the country's wealthiest citizens, but the dominant style has moved on from opulence to a cleaner, classic look – as in the work of Mrs Henry Parish II (*see* pp. 40–3), who designed for clients high on the American social register, including Astors, Whitneys and Vanderbilts, from the 1960s to the 1990s.

Throughout the 19th and 20th centuries, sumptuous interiors have been created to emulate styles from around the world – from red-lacquered formal Chinese rooms to relaxed North African bazaars littered with rugs, silver and embroidered fabrics. Today, couturier Tomasz Starzewski, in collaboration with decorator Tessa Kennedy, has created a feast of decorative opulence in his London apartment, with colourful textured elements from all corners of the globe, including a varnished crumpled silver-paper finish to doors that recalls the corridor of gold at Russian Empress Catherine I's stunning summer palace in St Petersburg; the breathtaking palaces of pre-revolutionary Russia remain an inspiration for current designers and decorators working with extravagance in mind and rich materials at their fingertips. Although few decorators now create purely opulent interiors – partly because of the expense – the noble houses of many countries and eras set the stage from which today's imaginative designs have evolved.

Below: Jacques Garcia has enthusiastically restored his magnificent chateau from the Louis XIV epoch, Champ-de-Bataille, which includes this billiard room. On the wall is a Brussels tapestry representing the signs of the zodiac. The billiard lamp is Garcia's own design.

Jacques Garcia

"Why do simple when you can do complicated? Why do less when you can do more – much more? I wish to give elements of richness to everyone."

Jacques Garcia's knowledge of historical detail seems boundless. But his work is not a blatant copy of the past, more a reinvention of history. "Clients often wish to integrate objects in a time period, to reproduce its spirit, while keeping a living projection through time that condemns rigid museum style." The Frenchman's wit and irreverence combine to create exciting, rich and larger-than-life environments, with the atmosphere of the *grand siècle* but suited to the rigours of 20th-century life.

Left: An exotic and welcoming neo-Chinese bathroom has been redesigned entirely by Garcia, using panels of *laque de Cormandel* lacquer from the 18th century. In the foreground is a "*confidente*" chair, a design similar to a love seat; this model – also Garcia's own creation – is upholstered in 19th-century fabric.

Born in Paris in 1947, Garcia trained at the *Ecole Nationale Supérieure des Métiers d'Art* before starting with a firm where he specialized in contemporary architecture, achieving recognition for interiors of the Montparnasse Tower and the Meridien and Sofitel hotels in Paris. In the mid-1970s, he set up on his own, eventually acquiring grand clients who let him create the sumptuous and colourful "living" rooms of his dreams. "We are always in need of rooms with warmth and conviviality."

Decorator and designer, Garcia is as at home refurbishing museums (Paris's Carnavalet Museum of local history, Deauville's Strasburger Museum) as creating casinos or hotels in New York, Baden-Baden or Beirut. Key projects have included the

Hôtel Costes, near the Place Vendôme in Paris (in 1995), with its cosy *fin-de-siècle* dining room; and the exotic Ladurée tea room on the Champs Elysées (in 1998). His work ranges from displays at the Paris Antique Dealers' Biennale – a Chinese pagoda, an Egyptian temple – to a replica of a chateau for a collector of 18th-century furniture in Houston, Texas. Commissions include an Art Nouveau house in France for Carole Laure and Lewis Furey, an estate for Count and Countess de Witt in Switzerland, and a huge property in Russia. In 1998, Garcia worked on the Sultan of Brunei's Paris house on the Place Vendôme. All furniture and objects were newly made: "Many artisans were kept in business for two years by this project alone. Using quality craftsmen is an integral part of what I do and I am thrilled to have offered them an opportunity to work with such fine materials." Lapis lazuli was used in quantity in one room, as were other materials usually prohibitively expensive even for wealthy pockets.

For his own use, Garcia restored the Paris mansion of Louis XIV's architect, Jules-Hardouin Mansart, and the Château de Menou in Burgundy, before buying the Château du Champ-de-Bataille in 1992. His most passionate project, this 17th-century Normandy chateau lies 60 miles northwest of Paris. Encountering the chateau on a boyhood trip with his father, Garcia vowed to own it one day. The restoration was a herculean undertaking: in 1982 the government had refused to accept the enormous property as a gift to the nation, and it had fallen into severe disrepair.

The first task was to restore the proportions of the rooms, before embarking on stucco, pillars, tapestries and frescoes. The great *lit à la duchesse* alone

required over 2,000 hours of work by craftsmen to restore its silk embroideries overlaid with gold and silver fillets. Then came the playful elements. One room contains a pastiche of *The Arabian Nights*: carved wooden columns from Rajasthan around a deep rectangular pool, walls lacquered purple and blue, and a subtle celadon-green ceiling. The floor above is inspired by Czarist Russia.

Garcia is absorbed in the mood of the 18th century, yet is not afraid to incorporate the new or "fake." He feels that many great houses are restored to ill effect because pedantic restorers introduce objects only from the date of the house. "I did not set out to do another Versailles. Results can look phony, even when elements are authentic. I wanted to create the atmosphere of a place where generations had left their mark, down to the smallest detail – travel souvenirs and family pictures." His contribution to national historic monuments has been recognized by the award of the prestigious *Légion d'Honneur* from the French government.

Left: The richness of a neo-Gothic bedroom by Garcia comes from use of antiques, an exuberant colour scheme and varied textures. The interior is made of 19th-century *boiseries*, and the door covered in two-tone studded velvet. **Above right:** One of the vast bathrooms at Champ-de-Bataille has an alcove lined in 18th-century chintz. The ivory chairs are late 18th-century Anglo-Indian, and the Marilyn Monroe picture is by Hubert Le Gall.

An opulent interior in good taste requires dedication on the part of both the decorator and the client to find the best materials, along with uncompromising standards with regard to craftsmanship, and a reasonably high budget. Materials may be costly but are good value since their lifespan will probably be greater than ours. The sample board (*right*) shows elements typical of Jacques Garcia's designs, here in a drawing room belonging to Paris fashion designers.

Curtaining

Heavy curtains were invaluable in the days before efficient heating. In the 20th century they can still provide warmth, but also create an atmosphere of richness and comfort. "Damas Tournelle" **(1)**, a damask by fabric manufacturer Lelièvre, is lined with pink silk **(2)**. Tie-backs are indispensable when curtains are heavy; these excellent tassels **(3)** and fringes or *passementerie* are from Wemyss Houlés.

Soft furnishings

The padded banquette and chairs with buttons, designed by Garcia, are upholstered in the same gold damask as the curtaining and finished with rope fringe **(4)**.

Wall decor

Opting for a soothing match between walls and soft furnishings, Garcia has used gold damask to line the upper wall section **(5)**. The wall below has been hand-stamped with a small geometric pattern.

Embellishment

The embroidered monogram suggests stateliness and personalizes the setting.

Design signatures

Jacques Garcia has great respect for the 18th and 19th centuries and the quality of their furniture. In a sumptuous Napoleon III salon in a predominantly neo-Gothic Paris apartment, he uses this inspiration to create an effect that is luscious, elegant, delicate-looking and comfortable. Although he produces luxurious interiors, Garcia's work is robust, and is characterized by a sense of what is fitting and a dislike of unnecessary exaggeration.

Period influence

Garcia's love of historical detail is evident in the Louis XV chairs, with their curved cabriole legs – the essence of Rococo. In this room they mix with buttoned armless easy chairs (designed for ladies, these are lower than the average chair, to make it easier to sit down in a long gown), which work well with the scale of the carved pieces. The buttoned banquette introduces an element of less formal seating than the embroidered counterparts behind it – this type of refined embroidery became fashionable in continental Europe from the reign of Louis XIV.

Quality

Garcia is guided by quality, whatever the period of the items he is dealing with. He utilizes the exceptional quality of French 18th- and 19th-century furniture (the work of skilled craftsmen catering to a demanding public) but has no hesitation in combining such pieces with high-quality newly-made work.

Scale

The designer has a strong sense of the importance of scale. His work shows his awareness that a room with underscaled furniture can make people look clumsy, while one with overscaled furniture may diminish human occupants and make them fade into the furnishings.

TERIOR DECORATION
CACHEMIRES

Alberto Pinto

"I've learned so much, and often have had to challenge the ideas and principles that I held to be true. And there's still so much I want to know."

Alberto Pinto is best known for his luxurious interiors, perhaps because his own home in Paris, overlooking the Quai d'Orsay on the banks of the Seine, is decorated in very lavish taste, "although I did not keep to a specific period throughout." Beyond the small doors in the *petite entrée,* with its marble floor and collections of 18th-century French and Italian engravings, there is a grand and historic air about the Pinto home. With a vaulted ceiling in the *grande entrée* and Ionic marble columns flanking the *grand salon* entrance, which is outfitted with a full-height wrought-iron *Directoire* door, greater riches are promised within. The idea is evident: monumentality. A fine Aubusson rug lines the floor of the *grand salon,* which exhibits an eclectic mix of European furniture in early-19th-century Russian style. The *Salon Jaune* boasts a quilted *toile de jouy* by Burger depicting the discovery of America on the walls, and black lacquer and Boulle chinoiserie furniture. The velvet-swathed dining room in a deep green has rocaille motifs and blue-and-white Chinese porcelain on the table. A Napoleonic-style bed with scrolling cygnets holds court in Pinto's bedroom, which also contains his personal

Left: Red is a favourite colour for Pinto. In his small drawing room adjacent to the *grand salon*, criss-cross velvet ribbons create a quilted appearance on the walls covered in "*Les Amériques*" *toile de jouy* by Burger. The 18th-century Spanish chairs, covered in the same fabric, have their motifs highlighted by borders of green bouclé ribbon.

collections of treasured artifacts – rock crystals (he believes in their good-luck powers) and ruby Baccarat vases.

Prior to his current grand surroundings, Pinto occupied a vast Paris apartment near the Champ de Mars in which the author Paul Morand and his wife, Princess Soutzo, had lived for more than 30 years spanning the 1930s, '40s and '50s. Taken to the apartment by a client who then decided against moving in, Pinto was unable to forget the sheer proportions of the space, and moved there in 1978. It has been said that there is an uncanny resemblance between the eponymous hero of Morand's *L'Homme pressé* and Alberto Pinto. There has also been a suggestion that Pinto enjoys soaking up the souls of his homes' former occupants. His current home was previously occupied by Roger Vivier, the shoe designer, whose talent the decorator greatly admires.

Alberto Pinto began designing interiors in the 1960s. Running his own photography agency, specializing in architecture and design, brought him into contact with *Maison Française*, *Elle* magazine and others, which stimulated an interest in the field. He began to create projects in line with the prevailing trends of Functionalism – kinetic art hung on neon-lit walls, with plastic sculptural furniture and vivid geometric patterns. By the 1970s, he was fully established as a decorator.

Since then, he has moved on to create custom-designed homes worldwide that combine abundance with elegance. Generally viewed as a sophisticated professional, someone who understands quality and will never compromise, Pinto designs interiors that feature discreet comfort and privacy, along with orchestration on a grand scale. His work covers a wide variety of projects: "The list at the moment includes the largest French sailboat, two aircraft, four office buildings, an exhibition, a couple of summer houses and private homes in Geneva, Paris, New York and Brazil," he quietly recounts.

Above: In a Paris apartment, the master bathroom is entirely finished in "marble" stucco. The doors, as well as the bathroom furniture, are in marquetry inspired by 17th-century Dutch mirrors. **Right:** The *Salon Bleu* is in the style of Louis XVI, with chairs signed Tilliard and paintings by Hubert Robert framed in marble, in Louis XVI tradition. The large vase is alabaster, and the table is designed by Cabinet Pinto.

PARIS

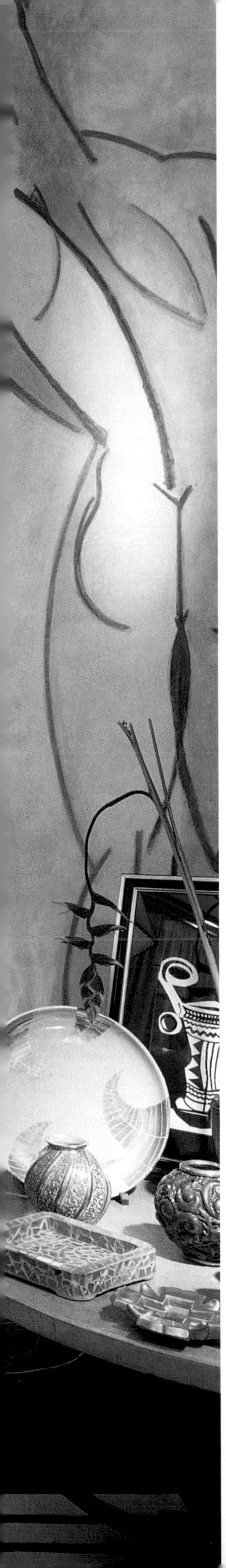

"I am remembered for my opulent interiors but, frankly, this is not all I do. Some of my projects are very contemporary. It is the skill of the people working within this profession to adapt to many styles from many periods to suit the clients' wishes. It does not necessarily always mean we end up with an eclectic interior. I am referring to versatility, and of course the rooms have to work for the individual." Even Pinto's more modern interiors evoke a warm but epic feel that is uniquely his own. On New York's Wall Street, the office lobby of a long-established firm needed the hand of Alberto Pinto to create an interior that would echo the stability and permanence of the firm and its reputation. Now, a clock measuring 12ft (4m) in width presides over the 90ft- (30m-) high marble-clad space. Five globes representing the five continents sit atop simple consoles supported by granite spheres in monumental fashion. The look, while undeniably epic and grand, is at the same time ultra-modern.

Much of Pinto's style owes its origins to his Moroccan roots. His childhood was unremarkable: he was "a calm, well-behaved child growing up in an uncomplicated family." The family home was particularly large, which may account for the designer's love for wide-open, almost gigantic interior spaces. His passion for entertaining also developed during his youth in the Moroccan city of Casablanca, where he remembers constant comings and goings of family and friends. The need for colour and warmth comes from his love of the Moroccan climate – cold interiors are banished from his world in favour of comfort. His interest in things foreign dates from his youth, too: in post-colonial Casablanca, Paris had a powerful influence on taste and it was normal to prefer the far-away French to the local Moroccan style.

Pinto's designs are largely guided by his instincts. Travel led him to capture what he enjoys in "French elegance, British chic and American rationalism." From the Orient he extracts pomp; a favourite is the Orient in European and especially in French interiors. His penchant for Russian furnishings, particularly those from the 19th century, has led him to create delightfully nostalgic decors. He adores daring juxtaposition and has developed a style which appeals to an international clientele who lean toward the eclectic.

His decorating philosophy involves creating an illusion of space. He then turns things around: cosy boudoirs take on elements of a grand drawing room, and *grands salons* forget to be so grand, allowing intimate gatherings of close friends. Pinto believes he is simply the "organizer of daily life" for his clients. Rather than creating new styles, a passion of the 20th century, he is content to remodel older ones, in his subtle manner. Styles from different geographical origins and eras are mixed and reinterpreted with a modern twist.

Left: The Cocteau Suite in Pinto's Paris apartment was inspired by his collection of lithographs and ceramics by the painter-poet Jean Cocteau. Dominique F. Derive created the frescoes which encircle the suite. On a table beside the sharkskin bed is a collage by Yves St Laurent and a 1960s plate. **Above right:** Accessorizing the fur bedcover is a monkey-face pillow made from a rare 19th-century antique silk-velvet fabric.

CLASSIC

Good interior decoration in the traditional or classic style re-creates a historical period from a contemporary view-point, without sacrificing its gracious quality and livableness for the sake of functionalism. Rooms are modern in that they have convenient and efficient arrangements of furniture, are bright and refreshing with sophisticated colour schemes, and are finely conceived. Decorators' main efforts, when working in this vein, usually focus on interpreting trends discriminately and designing original interiors that are based on historical period inspiration.

Above: The bedroom in the late Geoffrey Bennison's flat in Audley Square in London's Mayfair, where he lived from 1981 until 1984, when the fabric and furniture company Bennison was formed. The mahogany four-poster bed designed by Bennison is still produced today.

Previous pages: The Yellow Room at Avery Row, London, by American-born decorator Nancy Lancaster (who lived there for a time), epitomizes classic English style. In this room of perfect proportion, yellow silk-taffeta curtains are by John Fowler, and bookcases in front of the Venetian mirrors support Mason's ironstone pots – the fashion for placing large pots up high to balance architectural scale derives from the 18th century.

There was a time when rooms were reproduced in their entirety from French chateaux, Italian palazzos and fine English houses (in the early years of the 20th century, American millionaires even sought to express prestige and power by using professional decorators to re-create Renaissance palaces), but the interior decorator today is more likely to be concerned with the minor details of a period. The effect loosely described as 18th century is popular, and various renderings of the scheme come and go, changing with the decades. In some cases, 18th-century styles have been interpreted with rare antiques, costly interior treatments and luxurious fabrics, but the same effect can be achieved more economically by using the right colourful backgrounds with simple furniture and accessories. Pattern upon pattern can be used, but never in too strident a manner that endangers harmony; grand pieces can be combined with simple elements to great effect.

"A good background to be comfortable in," is how Jean Monro, daughter of and successor to Mrs Monro (who set up her decoration firm in London in 1926), describes the classic look the firm has become known for. The 18th century is her passion: "I was brought up on Palladio," she says, having been schooled in Italy, "which is what the 18th century is all about as far as I am concerned. It's the most successful of all architectural styles for living in, because the proportions are so good. I've often seen houses of this period that have been able to rise above what's been done to them down the years." Characteristic of the period are the qualities of fine craftsmanship, restraint and good taste. In tackling a historic interior, according to Jean Monro, it is necessary to be diligent in "doing the homework" and recognize when to stop.

Decorating as a profession was born in the 20th century. Traditionally, it had been the architect, retailer, upholsterer or cabinet-maker who advised on the arrangement of interiors. However, in the years leading up to World War I, decorating emerged as an acceptable profession for women: because of the consultative nature of the work – the role of the decorator is one of confidant and adviser – women found themselves able to lead and to excel. This extension of a traditional women's role into professional practice had its conception in the United States, where women were generally less restricted than in Europe by established codes of behaviour. It was aided by people like textile designer Candace Wheeler (1827–1923), who established the New York Society of Decorative Art in 1877 to educate women needing outlets for their handicraft.

In 1897, the architect Ogden Codman, Junior and future novelist Edith Wharton collaborated on the book *The Decoration of Houses*, which catapulted the notion of interior decoration as a profession into public consciousness. Codman was interested in classical styles and Wharton was impressed by the architects Charles McKim and Stanford White, who pioneered a close working relationship between architects and designers of the interior. Wharton and Codman believed that for too long people had been building up gaudy ornament and superficial effects in their houses and, in their manifesto claiming "house decoration as a branch of architecture," urged architects and decorators to pay heed to the spatial consequences of decorative decisions, guided by common sense and a respect for simplicity. The book set a precedent for all decorating activity from then on by equating "good taste" with English, Italian and French models from as far back as the Renaissance, with particular emphasis on the "Old French Look." The craft of the decorator became associated with elegant versions of antique interiors, and interior design was at once deemed a worthwhile undertaking.

However, it took a while for interior design to reach a wide market. "I think from the turn of the century to the 1930s, interior decorating was still just for the very rich – the people who hired Elsie de Wolfe, Syrie Maugham and Frances Elkins out in California, doing those huge houses for her brother, the architect David Adler," explained interior decorator Mark Hampton (*see* p. 31) in a lecture at Parsons School of Design, New York, in the early 1980s. "Decorating really started to become an enormous business after the Second World War, with people like William Pahlmann and all the magazines and the promotion."

Country-house styles

Although the earliest professional decorators were Americans, the traditional or classic interior created by design professionals has its history in both the United States and Europe. English country-house style seems to have little to do with the grand air of English country seats. The stateliness we recognize as the English country look is not as ancient as we might believe, but a product of the decorating profession that is less than a century old. It took the talent of great decorators from the 1920s onward, and a new generation of country-house owners, to turn neglected decoration into a covetable style with the appearance of having been put together over generations.

Many British clients who commissioned work from interior decorators in the middle of the 20th century lived in historic buildings and wanted to re-create or maintain the authenticity of an interior. The British decorator John Fowler (*see* pp. 34–9) understood paint colours and effects, finishes, floor coverings and curtaining, as well as being an authority on period furniture; he was thus a valuable expert whose popularity contributed to the success of the English country-house look, in part due to the frequent exposure of his projects in periodicals such as British *Country Life* (founded in 1897). Characteristic elements of Fowler's work, beyond decorative painting, included curtaining that was meticulously swagged, fringed and

Below: An antique French chair in Geoffrey Bennison's bedroom. He was a seminal influence in decorating, known for his English designs on muted background cloths. The drape fabric and wallpaper shown here, "Brown Roses," remains in production.

Above: A casual scheme by charismatic British interior designer Nicholas Haslam, who is well known for his elegant interiors on a grand scale, for clients including Hollywood actors and royalty. Here, the accent is on ease and comfort, a tenet of English country-house style.

tasselled; comfortable upholstery; pyramid bookcases; chandeliers; pairs of anything; and ubiquitous chintz in faded colours. His most popular chintz design was, and remains, "Old Rose." He used dyed-tape borders as an edge to such patterns as "Berkeley Sprig." Another Fowler innovation was the attachment of silk bows to the tops of picture-hanging cords at the cornice. He also showed a knack for creativity on a budget, especially during and after World War II, when rationing meant limited availability of materials. Dyed blankets, surplus noile from silk parachutes, and the purple-and-white fabric originally created for nurses' uniforms were all put to imaginative use.

In contrast to Fowler, who initially had little contact with affluence or aristocracy, other designers exploited their social connections to further their careers. Lady Sibyl Colefax gave legendary dinner parties at Argyll House in London's fashionable Chelsea to lure potential customers. Colefax had turned from life as a society hostess to become a professional decorator in 1933, after losing money in the Wall Street Crash. She enchanted clients and friends with her very English interiors, inspired by the chintz and solid furniture of the English country house. In 1938, Colefax took on Fowler as a partner. This proved an excellent choice, as Fowler was an expert on 18th-century decoration (although self-taught) and had a refreshingly down-to-earth approach in a world dominated by society women. For Fowler, the partnership brought access to grand houses, where he was motivated by the owners' respect for tradition. When Colefax retired in 1946, the business was bought by Nancy Lancaster (*see* p. 32), another society hostess. Her collaboration with Fowler, productive and irresistible if not always harmonious, enabled him to maximize his potential.

Both Fowler and Lancaster enjoyed the ease and comfort that come from a degree of informality, and believed that rooms should carry the "patina of life." Lancaster would take sofas into the garden to "bash about" in the elements to make them shabbier, while chintz was washed in tea to "age" it. The key was modesty and a belief that decoration is only a background to life.

This tenet of English country-house style, that it should be comfortable to live in, was also reflected on the other side of the Atlantic. Georgia-born Ruby Ross Wood (a journalist with American *Vogue* and *House & Garden* before turning decorator) as early as 1918 preached comfort as the governing idea behind her designs. Wood, who was responsible for creating the first decorating department, "Au Quatrième" in New York's Wanamaker's department store, was famous for her wit and charm as well as her colour-drenched rooms, and reportedly told a client who had come up with two decorating suggestions, "We will consider only the one that is most comfortable."

French country-house style, in contrast, is a formal and very conscious art, more ornate and less solid than the English, less comfortable and with fewer objects. It is elegant and disciplined, the result of artifice. The French approach is to take a room back to its architectural ornament and add few pieces of furniture. The result is polished and tight – more symmetrical than the English look.

American country-house style is strongly influenced by Europe, commonly adopting the more sumptuous and luxurious elements to create decorative rooms lyrical with light colour and gold, with ornate French chairs – altogether more flamboyant and "glossy" than in Europe. Whereas English and French styles favour faded grandeur and demure elegance – the British call it "shabby gentility" – the American preference tends to be extravagant (perhaps due to clients' larger budgets and a desire to reflect wealth). However, there is another faction of American country style with a more native approach, born out of the strong puritanical interiors of northern colonials and the Greek Revival period from the end of the 19th century. In this style, neoclassical pieces ornament less ostentatious rooms decked in rush matting, and taffetas alternate with unpretentious gingham fabrics according to the season. The result is country simplicity with grand and gracious ease.

Modern classics

Mark Hampton, who died in 1998, was world-famous for his traditional schemes with a modern edge and his ability to combine unfussy elements of English taste with the slickness of American. Having studied history, economics and law at London School of Economics, he changed career direction, working for David Hicks from 1961 in London and New York, then for McMillen Inc (*see* p. 33) and Sister Parish (*see* pp. 40–3), before setting up his own successful interior-design firm in New York. In the early 1980s, at the peak of the fashion for the traditional English look in the United States, he explained the relationship between taste and the new fashion: "I've been in New York for 18 years. I've seen decorators like Mrs Henry Parish and McMillen Inc go from very conservative, beautiful, valuable-looking rooms to rooms that are much more strongly stated. Taste is much more adventuresome now. The McMillen canons of taste were, and are, very strict. I read a very appropriate line by Nancy Lancaster in a recent magazine saying that you don't want to do everything up and get it finished down to the last detail. Something has to be left undone. Those McMillen rooms of the 1930s and '40s had a wonderful coolness to them. They weren't completely fringed up or gilded, and the mouldings weren't excessive." Whatever the taste of the time, it is the balanced blend of ease, restraint and grandeur that marks a classic interior.

Below: A contemporary drawing room by Wendy Nicholls of the firm Sibyl Colefax & John Fowler shows a modern take on tradition. Traditional elements, the hallmarks of the style developed by Colefax and Fowler in postwar years, provide a soft backdrop for a sophisticated art collection.

Nancy Lancaster

Below: Nancy Lancaster posed for Cecil Beaton in the hall at Haseley Court. The house had a Georgian core, with a Gothic Revival library on one side and a two-storied neoclassical salon on the other.

Born into a distinguished American family from Virginia, Nancy Lancaster was educated in France and the United States, before a trip to England in 1915 to stay at Cliveden in Buckinghamshire with her aunt, Nancy Astor. A second visit took place in 1919 (its aim was to help Nancy get over the death of her first husband, Henry Field – on the ship she met her late husband's cousin, Ronald Tree, who was to become her second husband). At Cliveden the young Nancy watched as her aunt breathed life into the house.

Nancy and Ronald Tree began their married life in the United States, renting a house on East 96th Street, New York, from Ogden Codman (architect and co-author, with Edith Wharton, of the book *The Decoration of Houses*, *see* pp. 28–9). They then acquired Mirador, Nancy's family house in Virginia, which she began to decorate according to a mixture of nostalgic whim and inherent skill – using, among other devices, old chintz to create an effective time-weathered appearance.

In 1926 the Trees moved to Britain, leasing first Cottesbrooke, then Kelmarsh Hall, both in Northamptonshire. Just before World War II, they bought Ditchley Park and its 3,000-acre estate in Oxfordshire; like Kelmarsh, it had been built by James Gibb, a prominent 18th-century English architect. Nancy's sensitive restoration of the two Gibb houses, and her work on their gardens, gained her recognition as an outstanding talent in the years before the war. During the war, Winston Churchill often visited Ditchley, as it was not considered a likely target for German bombing raids.

After the war was over, the Trees' marriage ended, and Nancy briefly married the owner of Kelmarsh, Claude "Jubie" Lancaster. (She once quipped that she preferred houses to husbands, on the basis that they "last longer.")

When Sibyl Colefax retired from Colefax and Fowler (*see* pp. 34–9), due to ill health, Nancy Lancaster acquired the business. John Fowler's career was still in its infancy when they met. Socially, their backgrounds were very different: Lancaster was a society hostess familiar with the grandeur of great country houses and American wealth, whereas Fowler was completely unfamiliar with the aristocracy and such affluent clients.

Together, in 1954, they embarked on a superb restoration of the near-derelict Haseley Court in Oxfordshire (where Nancy was to live for the rest of her life, at first in the main house, then, from 1975, in the Coach House). Fowler, adept at decorating rooms, created the soft furnishings, while the rooms' conception and the furniture selection were the result of Lancaster's imagination. She would blend the fine with the characterful and, according to Cecil Beaton, had "a healthy disregard for the sanctity of important pieces." Her American influence on English country-house style was profound – she even insisted on comfortable, warm bathrooms in all houses she set her hand to, adding them *en suite* to increase the bathroom-to-guest ratio – while her knowledge of French and Italian furniture and decoration helped shape the cross-cultural future of the look originally conceived by Colefax and Fowler. It was said she had a maverick eye and exquisite taste.

In 1957, with Colefax and Fowler seemingly on the brink of financial ruin, it was decided to turn the salon at the back of the firm's offices at 39 Brook Street, in London's Mayfair, into a studio. Fowler and Lancaster collaborated again on the project. Now known as the Yellow Room (*see* p. 26) at Avery Row, the most famous of London drawing rooms, the "studio" they created is easy and comfortable – yet has the grandeur of an Italian palazzo.

BIOGRAPHY

1897	Born in Albemarle County, Virginia.
1914	Orphaned.
1915	Attended Foxcroft school, Middleburg, Virginia.
1916	Debutante, New York.
1919	Married Ronald Tree.
1926	Moved to Britain.
1933	Bought Ditchley Park, Oxfordshire.
1946	Acquired Colefax and Fowler.
1950s	Worked closely with John Fowler.
1954	Bought Haseley Court, Oxfordshire.
1957	Created the Yellow Room at Avery Row, London, with Fowler.
1994	Died.

Eleanor Brown

Eleanor Brown (born Eleanor Stockstrom in 1890; after marriage she became Eleanor McMillen and then, with her second marriage in 1935, Eleanor Brown) was originally from St Louis, Missouri, in the American Midwest. She founded McMillen Inc in New York in 1924 as "the first professional full-service interior-decorating firm in America."

Brown worked within the classical idiom. She held that "Man is still a creature requiring comforts and even luxuries, of a rather prescribed and traditional nature." However, she also valued the time in which she lived: "Love of beauty and the desire to create it is a primal instinct. It is right that we should wish to live in a manner that is in keeping with our own time in history." Brown had taken classes in art history and business practice, and had trained at the New York School of Fine and Applied Arts and at Parsons School of Design in Paris, under one of the founders, William Odom. She was determined not to be identified with the somewhat amateurish approach of many of her contemporaries who were simply decorators. To Brown, architecture held the key to a scheme. She was perhaps the foremost exponent of the philosophy of decoration introduced by Edith Wharton and Ogden Codman in the first American book on interior design, *The Decoration of Houses* (published in 1897), which can be summed up by the idea that the habits of daily life should be ritualized by "suitable," preferably classical, rooms suggesting dignity and nobility of spirit. She felt that progress depends on "knowledge based on tradition plus an imaginative and sensitive concept of a private world."

Typical McMillen Inc interiors use acid yellow to offset symmetrically placed antique and satin-upholstered furniture in rooms often containing contemporary paintings and sculpture. "Old patterns seem excitingly fresh when rejuvenated by a contemporary palette," according to Brown. Black-and-white checked floors and other geometric floor patterns feature heavily: "I believe in simplicity and restraint." Clients at McMillen Inc included Mr and Mrs Henry Parish II, and the Rockefeller, Winthrop, Aldrich and Lorillard families.

Over a period of 40 years, Brown, a trustee of Parsons School in New York, hired almost exclusively Parsons graduates. In 1926 she employed Grace Flakes, and in the late 1930s, Marian "Tad" Morgan. Brown retired on her 88th birthday. Today Betty Sherrill is at the helm of McMillen, which has trained a number of legendary decorators, including Nathalie Davenport, Mark Hampton (*see* p. 31), Albert Hadley (*see* pp. 72–7) and Tom Buckley, in its 75 years in business.

BIOGRAPHY

1890	Born in Missouri.
1924	Founded McMillen Inc, New York.
1927	First public exhibition, New York Exposition of Architecture and Applied Arts.
1930s	Taught at Parsons School, New York.
1932	"Interiors of Tomorrow" exhibition of miniature rooms (with Grace Flakes), in various North American cities.
1940	Opened first branch of McMillen Inc in Houston, Texas.
1943	Acquired and began decorating a former theatre in Long Island.
1973	Decorated a room at the first Kips Bay show house, Manhattan.
1991	Died.

Left: In Eleanor Brown's apartment on the East River, New York (her home from 1928 onward), the neoclassical oval dining room has a green-and-white marble floor, an English Regency table and leather-covered French *Directoire* chairs.

John Fowler

"John Fowler had 'it,' whatever 'it' is. Like Charles Beistegui and a very few others, John understood beautiful things and was drawn to them like a moth to a flame. I think it must be something born into you, this love for beauty." Nancy Lancaster

John Fowler, of the English decorating firm Colefax and Fowler, was a prolific interior decorator, both of private houses and for the National Trust in Britain. One of the most influential figures of the 20th century in period decoration, he adapted many designs from 18th- and early-19th-century fragments of wallpapers and textiles. After his death, his work continued through top decorators Stanley Falconer, Roger Banks Pye and Imogen Taylor; today the Colefax and Fowler look is re-created for modern tastes by Wendy Nicholls and Vivien Greenock.

Fowler, born in 1906, worked at a bank, a printers and an estate agents before a year in the countryside that taught him to love simple beauty. In the 1920s he began to paint Chinese wallpaper at Thornton Smith's Soho studio in London. There he caught the attention of the antique dealer and decorator Margaret Kunzer, who hired him and, in 1931, put him in charge of a furniture-painting studio for the department store Peter Jones.

It was a time of change for Fowler. Moving from his mother's home to a rented house in King's Road, Chelsea (opposite Syrie Maugham [*see* p. 63] and Sibyl Colefax), he wore long hair,

Left: At first, the owner disliked the wall colour in this drawing room in an English manor house, decorated by Fowler in 1955, but Fowler insisted the shade would fade within two years, then rest; it did, and for over 30 years the apricot paint remained the same. The room's colours were composed around the Aubusson rug shades: Bordeaux red, and sage and other greens.

On a first trip to Paris, he was impressed by the quality of decorative objects at fleamarkets, and by the French use of paint: mauves, grays, off-whites, yellows and bluer reds. He also discovered hand-block-printed papers with motifs mainly from the 19th century, and learned to incorporate "a dash" of delicate French furniture in room designs to offset more severe English forms.

In 1938, Sibyl Colefax took on Fowler as a partner. During World War II, he was exempted from military service because of delicate health and poor eyesight, but enlisted as a fire warden, working for the business on his one day off each week. In 1944, the offices moved to 39 Brook Street, Mayfair. When Colefax retired, the business was bought by Nancy Lancaster (*see* p. 32).

Postwar years found Fowler decorating rooms at Buckingham Palace and for Lord Rothermere at Daylesford. Restorations included 44 Berkeley Square, London (designed by William Kent), the Adam interiors of Syon House, Middlesex, and James Wyatt's cloisters at Wilton House, Wiltshire. Fowler's work for the National Trust, from 1956, was some of his greatest. After retiring from Colefax and Fowler in 1969 with cancer-related problems, he devoted his remaining years to the restoration of over 25 National Trust houses.

All his life, Fowler was a professional artisan supporting himself by his work. But he is best remembered at home in his modest hunting lodge in Odiham, Hampshire, purchased in 1947. Its decoration was a challenge, continually refined until his death in 1977: "What I wanted here was something utterly unpretentious, very comfortable, with a veneer of elegance and informality."

baggy clothes and sandals, and gave many parties. He met a new circle of artistic friends, including the Sitwell brothers, Michael and Rachel Redgrave and Laurence Olivier, some of whom would become his clients. Hours were spent in the Victoria and Albert Museum, studying costume detail and furniture (the ruffled taffeta curtains he made in the 1950s for Mrs David Bruce, the US ambassador's wife, can be traced to the hem of an 18th-century costume). Brighton Pavilion was also an inspiration. He studied drapery in design books by the French Baroque designer Daniel Marot and was absorbed by music, ballet and theatre.

In 1934 Fowler left Peter Jones to set up his own painting studio in Smith Street, Chelsea; always popular, he took with him five of his staff. Later that year, he established a decorating business, using the King's Road house as a showroom. Projects included rooms at Blenheim Palace in Oxfordshire.

Fowler termed his look "humble elegance." Where others used porcelain, he would choose creamware or pottery. He would select a Regency painted chair or blond-wood commode over Queen Anne walnut or carved mahogany Chippendale.

Above left: A London drawing room for the US ambassador's wife drew its design from a Louis XVI prototype. The clock and painting are attached by a ribbon and bow; curtain edges were scalloped using nail scissors.
Right: The sitting room for Pauline de Rothschild in the Albany, on London's Piccadilly, has oyster silk-taffeta curtains, cut with pinking shears. Turquoise Ionic pilasters, dado and skirting (baseboard) are painted to simulate marble.

From his early decorating days, John Fowler constantly sought fragments of old wallpapers and fabrics to use as inspiration for new designs. He found "Old Rose" and "Brompton Stock," two favourite chintzes, in the archives of the company Warners in the 1950s. It was Fowler's successors, Tom Parr and George Oakes, who began to use such scraps as a basis for fabric collections, which have been in production since 1968. Some of the early samples were found at Coles' factory in Islington, London, others in drawers and cupboards in grand houses. Here, in Tom Parr's house in France, the accent is on comfort and simplicity, but the walls and floors are not bare.

Wallpaper

The walls are papered in "Colefax Trellis" in blue **(1)**. The move from interior to exterior is gentle: French doors are welcoming and the wallpaper pattern evokes the *treillage* of a garden room.

Upholstery

The armchair is upholstered in a glazed cotton fabric, "Gallica," in apricot **(2)**. Rose-pink piping **(3)** neatens off the edges of the upholstery.

Curtaining

The curtains have been made to match the chair, with bobbled fringing to finish – here, the samples are from Wendy Cushing **(4)**.

Floor covering

A simple needlework Portuguese rug **(5)** brings a country rusticity to the room.

Mirrors

A pair of oval mirrors **(6)** flank the French doors.

Design signatures

The spirit of John Fowler still abounds. His influence is spread particularly through the good reputation of employees and former employees of the firm, who included George Oakes and Imogen Taylor at first; later Stanley Falconer, Roger Banks-Pye and Tom Parr (none of whom are with the company now), and others, like Wendy Nicholls and Vivien Greenock, who remain under the Sibyl Colefax & John Fowler banner.

The English country look

Fowler's serious approach to decorating had always been applauded by the firm's private clients, for whom he would create homes for living, but public recognition of the company came initially through the reputation of the Brook Street shop in London, with its atmosphere of refined country charm. Colefax and Fowler seemed like a country cousin, in the nicest sense, with its quiet taste, modest antiques and painted furniture – functional but attractive pieces. It was Tom Parr, who eventually succeeded John Fowler as principal decorator at Colefax and Fowler, who initiated the retailing of the stock items and who made the brave move to open the Chintz Shop in Ebury Street, London, and the many retail outlets throughout Britain and internationally. At Colefax and Fowler, Tom Parr seemed to understand accessibility and to have an astute sense of what the public wanted: rooms of our own time but embodying the spirit of the past.

Balance and proportion

The country look is underpinned by a classic elegance. Furniture is often paired, the rules of proportion are adhered to in curtain treatments (pelmets or valances being one-third of the drop), and smaller pictures are grouped symmetrically, often linked with a ribbon-and-bow finish.

Sister Parish

"If my 'undecorated look' has meant rooms that are personal, comfortable, friendly and gay, I feel I have accomplished a great deal.... Rooms should be 'timeless.' If I can create a 'living' room, that is true success."

Mrs Henry Parish II, of the New York firm Parish-Hadley Associates, believed in comfort and practicality. Born Dorothy May Kinnicutt in Morristown, New Jersey, in 1910, she was nicknamed "Sister" by one of her brothers. Her upbringing was privileged. Only after education, social debut and marriage to Henry Parish II, a Harvard-educated stockbroker like her father, did Sister turn to decorating. Her parents' good taste (her father was a furniture connoisseur) informed her work, and she went on to decorate homes for prominent Americans, including William Paley and his style-mogul wife, Babe; Brooke Astor; Gordon and Ann Getty; Mr and Mrs John Hay Whitney; and Happy Rockefeller. Her distinguished career won her many friends and impressive commissions, the most famous of which was the restoration of the White House in Washington, DC, for President and Mrs Kennedy in the early 1960s.

Sister Parish's work showed intuitive understanding of luxurious comfort (she could create easy seating for 30 people in a modest-sized sitting room); her style was to become synonymous with classic American elegance. Untrained, and no follower of trends, she relied on her own preferences:

Left: The entrance hall of Sister Parish's New York maisonette (formerly Gloria Swanson's) has linen-covered walls, painted in freehand stripes and crowned with a *Directoire* border. On the bleached-oak parquet floor is a Bessarabian rug; 18th-century side chairs are covered in cocoa silk. On top of the clock is a curtain finial for extra height. The chandelier is Russian.

glazed chintzes (she is associated with Lee Jofa's chintz "Floral Bouquet and Border"); painted furniture; woven rugs and rich textiles; four-poster beds and knitted throws. A champion of American crafts, she avoided formality while assuring quality.

One influence was Sibyl Colefax: "I learned the extraordinary art of understated British comfort from her. Luscious, mouth-watering glazed chintzes. I spread her gospel then added a few footnotes." Other influences were John Fowler (*see* pp. 29–30 and 34–9) and Nancy Lancaster (*see* p. 32).

Parish also considered "memory" important: "My first reaction, if I do not already know the person, is to try to feel out what he or she really wants the room to be and to understand what 'memory,' old or new, has brought this idea about."

Her own memories date from her parents' sitting room, which had twisted glass lamps with paper shades. "My father had made them, cutouts of lacy designs of flowers, birds and clouds. I remember my mother saying, 'Please put a wash of pale pink inside them.' Years later in Paris I was to hear these same words of advice echoed. Madame Ritz herself conducted me on a tour of the Ritz Hotel. She said to me, 'In doing a room, you have only one rule to remember: always line your lampshades with pale pink.'" Pink-lined lampshades became one of Parish's hallmarks.

She decided to take up decorating while on honeymoon in Paris in 1930. In their first house, the Parishes "put white-striped paper on the walls and used white mattress ticking for the curtains. The bed was covered with white silk-taffeta with borders of flowers. Above the head of the bed this taffeta drapery flowed downward from a crown. I remember that the first night we spent there we kept the lamps lit because it was so beautiful."

Professional work followed. Early in Parish's career, she designed the timeworn interiors of the Essex Hunt Club in New Jersey. When World War II took Henry Parish to the Pacific, Sister moved to New York, took up Red Cross work, and joined the firm Budget Decorators. In 1948, she and Bunny Mellon (a friend from Foxcroft school in Virginia) discussed possible collaboration with the English firm Colefax and Fowler (*see* pp. 30 and 34–9), but the project was halted by currency restrictions.

In 1962, after 28 years in business, Parish met Albert Hadley (*see* pp. 72–7), through Van Day Truex (*see* p. 73), design director of Tiffany. Despite their very different talents – Parish evoking family and permanence, Hadley the chic and modern – they became partners in 1964. Parish-Hadley served almost as a graduate school for decorators: its alumni included Mark Hampton (*see* p. 31), David Easton, Keith Irvine, Bunny Williams and David Kleinberg. Sister Parish continued to live and work until the age of 84.

Above left: In a home for a client with a passion for English country houses, a four-poster canopy bed, flanked by a pair of English japanned chests, and a wheel-back Hepplewhite settee stand on a paisley-patterned carpet. **Right:** Off-white damask sofas, pink-painted walls and an Aubusson rug soften Parish's drawing room. Beside the fireplace are English Regency girandoles; above it a 1930s portrait of Parish, painted by Edward Murray.

Mario Buatta

"In the old days, architects put in mouldings, fancy windows, even pediments and columns. Today buildings are devoid of all embellishments – one has to start from scratch. But although I do all those things, I think of myself as an old-fashioned decorator."

Dubbed the "Prince of Chintz," Mario Buatta creates decors that evoke interiors of the 18th and 19th centuries. His signature is extensive use of flowered and coated fabrics; he insists on a move toward soft-edged romance, simplified for a new kind of living. "It seems to me that people are heading back to a more stable environment after a period of experimentation with new materials and styles," he said in an article written in 1982. "It is now clear that well-made 18th- and 19th-century things can age better than plastics – yet they can also contribute to a very contemporary look."

Left: The library of a New York triplex apartment decorated by Buatta in the late 1980s has Prussian-blue glazed walls and a wall-to-wall ocelot-design carpet. The armchair is in a yellow chintz by Brunschwig & Fils; the carpet is Victorian needlework. The bow-and-sash device to hang the picture was inspired by John Fowler, who had seen it in 18th-century paintings.

New York-based Buatta, born in 1935, has built up an impressive client list over the years, including Henry Ford II and the US government – for the latter, he collaborated with decorator Mark Hampton (*see* p. 31) to design the interior of Blair House in Washington, DC, the state guesthouse for visiting dignitaries. Buatta has evolved a very personal style, and his clients tend to appreciate his sense of humour, freedom of expression and extensive use of colour. In 1982, he predicted, "Colour will become a far more important decorating tool. We are living in gray times and, especially in the cities, people want more colour

in their lives and are learning how to achieve it. Even architects are responding to this need."

A major inspiration for Buatta has been the work of his friend and mentor John Fowler (*see* pp. 29–30 and 34–9), along with that of Nancy Lancaster (specifically her Yellow Room at Avery Row in London, *see* pp. 26 and 32) and Keith Irvine (Fowler's assistant in the late 1950s, for whom Buatta worked briefly in New York). Buatta met Fowler in 1963, and went on to spend Christmas with Fowler and friends at Fowler's hunting lodge in England each year from 1964 until 1977. Buatta took up Fowler's dictum that things should have a "pleasing edge of decay" and that decoration should be "well behaved but free from too many rules ... a *fantaisie* expressing the personality of its owner." Having learned to interpret Fowler's look of "humble elegance" so prevalent in some English country houses, he went on to re-create the look in the United States and develop his own brand of "tasteful" decorating, although, as he stated in 1982, he believes, "It's easier to put your finger on what constitutes 'good design' than 'good taste.'"

Buatta's prolific designing extended to the creation of furniture and fabrics for mass production. His 1990 furniture collection is made by John Widdicomb; Fabriyaz took his fabrics, Revman Industries the bedlinens, Thimbelina the needlepoint, and Imperial Sterling the wallpaper designs. More diverse projects include home fragrance (with the company Aromatique) and lighting (Frederick Cooper).

Perhaps surprisingly, Buatta's childhood environment had little influence on his taste. The family home was far from a picture of "humble elegance;" his father was bandleader Phil Burton, and the family lived on Staten Island, New York, in a house that Buatta is keen to forget: "I was brought up in a very contemporary house my parents built in the 1930s and furnished with glass and steel and chrome." However, his aunt had a more positive impact, her English-country-style house being "filled with what I used to call Thomas Chickendale furniture and chinoiserie. I was just crazy about all of those things. My uncle was an architect and I was very much influenced by what he was doing, which was more traditional than contemporary."

The young Buatta began collecting aged 11, when he bought a Sheraton writing box (antique lap desk) for $12. He had a good eye – the desk was later priced at $4,000. Collections, along with chintz, are now a key element of his look: "Collecting is a very personal thing. It relates to your childhood, it is about insecurity, and about wanting more. I get a lot of happiness just sitting and looking at these things." Today his own Upper East Side Manhattan apartment is designed around

Above left: The mantelpiece in the corner of the dining room is English 18th-century pine. The mirror above it is gilt Chippendale. **Right:** The gilt dolphin table is 18th century; the carpets are faded 19th-century Aubusson. The table is French (a Chinese lacquered top on a French gilt bevelled frame), and the sofas are reminiscent of Syrie Maugham's work. The colour schemes are derived from the owners' Impressionist paintings.

THE AGE OF

collections, as well as objects of interesting historical provenance. "People ask if the things are family possessions. I say, 'Well, yes, but not my family.'"

Buatta has a refreshing irreverence toward his chosen profession. "A lot of us are ashamed of our real pasts and a lot of people don't want to be reminded of where they come from." So he creates "new pasts" for many clients, with rooms looking as if generations of family members have used the furniture and contemplated the collections: "Someone called it the 'instant heritage look.'" Not all his clients, however, need new pasts. "We decorators create the stage on which you live out your lives," he explains. "It doesn't make sense if you don't create the right background for the client."

Although Buatta attended Cooper Union, New York, to study architecture, he was more interested in how things looked than how a building was constructed: "I like to think of myself as an old-fashioned decorator, because I was weaned on the Syrie Maughams and the Elsie de Wolfes of that time. When I went to school back in the 1950s, they were the people we knew about."

It was while studying at Parsons School of Design, in Paris and New York, that he was awakened to use of colour. "Stanley Barrows, who was responsible for teaching a great many of the decorators you hear about today, took us to the Modern Museum in Paris, through the Matisse and Bonnard and Vuillard areas of the galleries. He said that if you don't understand these painters' use of colour, you'll never become good decorators. It was interesting to hear then and it stuck in my mind."

That first European trip with Parsons was also when he realized that in Britain a family may have lived in a house for seven or eight generations, building up very personal collections over as much as three centuries. In the United States, one family might move seven or eight times, new possessions replacing the old with each move.

These days Mario Buatta feels that American decorating too often considers status and money. It is more important, he thinks, to live around objects that mean something. If an apartment becomes a status symbol and not a place of comfort to live, this, in Buatta's terms, is "dysfunctional decorating." He explains, "If I want to read a book and have a drink, I need a good chair, a table to put my drink on and a lamp to read by. If it also looks wonderful then that is what decorating is about. So often, I see designers come up with a quirky room everyone thinks is fabulous. Sometimes the room might look revolutionary and idiosyncratic, but it just doesn't work.... I like things to be a bit worn out – like me." His aim is maximum comfort within an exuberant interior, resulting in what he terms an "undecorated look."

Much of his enjoyment comes from creating an environment to come home to: "I like bedrooms best. Most people spend more time there than they realize. Rooms should be growing, living things. No room is ever finished. I like to think of decorating a house as an artist paints a picture – perhaps a dab at a time on the canvas until the composition comes together."

"Decorating is a living art and is still quite unappreciated," he adds. "What is also wrong today is that many fashion people, designers and decorators are not taught the classics." But he feels new decorators such as David Kleinberg (former vice-president at Parish-Hadley), Stephen Sills and James Huniford (*see* pp. 82–7), and Jeffrey Bilhuber are doing good work, and believes, "We are moving toward a feeling of what people like Dior and Bill Blass have been about: both 'substance' and 'elegance.'"

Right: "What I tried to create were day rooms and night rooms; the clients entertain often in the evening. You walk from a pale butter-yellow hall into the drawing room with its aubergine glazed high-gloss sheen for drama," says Buatta. "This is a soft room." The Cornucopia chintz appears as Fowleresque curtains and covers a Radnor chair and ottoman in the morning room. The table is Chinese.

Nina Campbell

"Decorating has much more to do with confidence than taste, and certainly shouldn't be dependent on prevailing fashions. It's important to follow your heart and your eye. Decorating rules, like any rules, are made to be broken – I break them all the time."

To Nina Campbell, visual imagination is more important than matching fabrics – she brings together plaids, florals and chintzes, creating beautiful rooms in which diverse elements form a unified theme. A prime consideration is the room itself: the colour scheme is inspired by its function and qualities. She holds that scale of pattern is important, and that different scales (very large or small) work better together than the middle-sized: "Avoid the middle road in everything: in decorating, in life, in friends."

Left: This bedroom features a classic oval dressing table in blue cotton ("Fenway Court" by Campbell, also on the lampshade and antique candlestick lamps). Walls and curtains are in *toile de jouy* "Asticou," while the mahogany stool is upholstered in "Brag," a tartan by Campbell. The 1930s blue triptych mirror is Venetian.

London-based, Campbell has worked for such high-profile clients as the Queen of Denmark, the Duke and Duchess of York (decorating the only royal residence built in England in the 20th century, in Sunninghill, Berkshire – she was allowed to rummage through the cellars of Buckingham Palace for artifacts), Ringo Starr and Rod Stewart. She epitomizes the best in what has become known as good English taste. "The English are good at putting things together," she comments. Trained under John Fowler (*see* pp. 29–30 and 34–9), she has been established in her own right for over 25 years and employs more than 20 staff. Her delicate yet practical style, along with flair and humour, have earned her the prestigious American Fashion Award for

the "woman who has most influenced style internationally." She has also been appointed a Trustee of the Victoria and Albert Museum in London.

Campbell attracts both commercial and domestic commissions. She has refurbished two luxury hotels in central Paris (Le Parc Victor Hugo and the Hôtel de Vigny) and, with David Linley, the lobby of the Savoy Hotel in London. Her ability to adapt has earned her domestic projects in London, New York, Hong Kong and Moscow, beach houses in California and castles in Scotland.

Born on the last day of World War II, Nina Campbell was influenced by her mother's talent for budget decorating. "My mother bought a bolt of taffeta at a warehouse sale and dyed it acid yellow for our drawing-room curtains, which we took from house to house. I probably became a designer because I was incapable of doing anything else."

Boarding school in Ascot in the south of England, a spell in Paris, then a first job in the gift department at the General Trading Company (GTC), a store in London's Chelsea, was followed by a course in shorthand and typing, but she soon returned to the GTC to run the wedding-list department. After 18 months, she left to visit a grandmother in the United States, see New York and visit Jamaica. On her return, she was interviewed for the post of assistant to John Fowler; his response was, "You clearly know nothing! But why not start next week?" Although Campbell was more interested in parties at this point in her life, her few years at Colefax and Fowler undeniably shaped her future, and both Nancy Lancaster (*see* p. 32) and John Fowler were a great influence. "With some people you have only to shake their hand and you learn something. John was like that. He exuded knowledge." Campbell has in turn had an impact on Colefax and Fowler – while working for the firm, she was commissioned to redecorate part of Annabel's nightclub in London: "In John Fowler's room I had found a scrap of wallpaper I knew he had taken from the same address, 44 Berkeley Square, while he was redoing the Clermont club upstairs. He had kept the scrap of paper, a beautiful scrap, but had not had time to do anything with it." Campbell persuaded the club's owner, Mark Birley, to have the paper remade by Coles of Mortimer Street for use in the nightclub downstairs, and subsequently the design "Berkeley Sprig" became a trademark of Colefax and Fowler.

At the age of 22, Campbell set up her own business with a friend; an early project – "challenging and satisfying," although it took four years – was the 18-bedroom Cullen House in Banffshire, Scotland. Other commissions followed. When her partner left to go abroad, Campbell

Above left: A country-house bathroom has amethyst "Polesdon Check" wallpaper and "Pencraig" fabric at the window. The bamboo chair, in amethyst "Rummy" tartan, and the table are antiques. **Right:** The reception hall of a country house, home to a young family; Campbell's brief was to form a comfortable seating area from a potentially daunting entrance hall – the colour scheme pre-ordained by sienna marble pillars.

went into a retail business with Birley. Their London shop in Pimlico marketed "unashamed luxury," including linens from the Porthault company, bamboo bath racks, and candies from Fauchon, Paris. However, the decorating passion soon resurfaced: Birley had bought Mark's club in Mayfair, and together they embarked on its decoration.

Three business addresses later (all in Walton Street, in South Kensington, London), Campbell expanded into fabric printing: a favourite criss-cross design had been discontinued by the manufacturers Tissunique and, wanting to use it, she obtained permission to reprint. The collection progressed to include rose-patterned chintzes and trellis motifs based on old documents and shawls from the Alsace region of France.

Apart from John Fowler, whom she remembers as "deeply loved by all," and Mark Birley, "a perfectionist," the American decorator Elsie de Wolfe (*see* p. 62) – "the first professional interior designer" – had a profound, if more distant, influence on Campbell's career, inspiring her to pen an authoritative work, *Elsie de Wolfe – A Decorative Life*. Campbell has also written *Nina Campbell on Decorating*, defining classic English style and highlighting features of her own look.

More recently, she opened a second shop, Nina *bis*, marketing antiques as well as her own fabrics, wallpapers, trimmings and a newly launched carpet collection. (An astute businesswoman, Campbell creates two wallpaper and fabric collections each year, distributed by Osborne & Little, and licenses many of her own products.) The main shop, run by her daughter Henrietta, sells contemporary home accessories along with old favourites.

Above right: Campbell's mastery of detail shows in a skirted button-back chair in French cotton fabric – formal and pretty. **Left:** In this octagonal drawing room in a house in the country, the pillars and beams were dark wood: Campbell had woodwork painted in broken whites and the walls the colour of pink champagne. Furniture was restored and re-covered in rose pinks and sage green, taken from the colours of the armchair fabric.

"I enjoy anything I have time to do properly," she says. "You mustn't be afraid to put things together, and include an element of wit. A sense of humour is a key." Twice married and divorced, she has advised: "Husbands come and go, but for heaven's sake, hang on to your curtain maker!"

Campbell's public appeal (she lectures in Europe, Australia and the United States) is not just based on her knowledge and taste, but also on her "spark" and ability to awaken people to what defines a good English room in a world where "traditional" implies "fuddy-duddy." She uses brutally expressive words to describe decoration, talking of "butching" things up. Although known for her English look, she is fond of Gallic style and passionate about French fabrics (*toile de jouy* is a favourite; in her 19th-century white stucco villa, red *toile de jouy* has pride of place in her bedroom, supported by maple and satinwood furniture). Her home is luxurious but simple, discreet and comfortable – "I design for living." Nor is the contemporary trend anathema: "What Philippe Starck (*see* pp. 180–5) does is very exciting. I'd love to live in a Jonathan Reed room (*see* pp. 88–91), and I admire Michael Reeves; Reed and Reeves combine contemporary with warmth."

You Can't Take It With You
There Are No Pockets In.A Shroud
Today

ELEGANT

In the halcyon days of the early 20th century, before the First World War, a new, pared-down yet luxurious elegance found its way into interiors through many sources. In America it was spurred on by the teachings of Edith Wharton and Ogden Codman, followed by Elsie de Wolfe. In France, it was prompted by visionary *ensembliers* and designers with a sense of refined and simplified luxury. In Britain, home interiors were initially unchanged, but a fashion for a barer, cleaner but ultra-luxurious look evolved during the late 1920s – at first in public interiors such as hotel foyers and theatres.

Above: Decorator Frédéric Méchiche, an ardent traveller, blends eclectic elements together in his Paris apartment. The white-painted wall-panelling was taken from 18th-century Parisian houses. The Italian sofa dates from around 1800.

Previous pages: Elsie de Wolfe, the first to announce herself as a professional interior designer (her business card depicted a wolf holding a flower in its mouth), discovered the deserted Villa Trianon, near Versailles, on a trip to France in 1905 with Elisabeth Marbury. Its renovation was an ongoing project, but for decades the two women spent summers there, entertaining friends. Shown here is the sitting room.

Much of the pared-down lavishness of the first quarter of the 20th century originated with French designers: Louis Süe (1875–1968) and André Mare (1887–1932), André Groult (1884–1967), Francis Jourdain (1876–1958), Emile Ruhlmann (*see* p. 64) and Paul Iribe (1885–1935). Iribe tended to traditionalism, attacking modern art in a 1926 manifesto; yet he also had a sense of Modernism that inclined to the Baroque, and veneered his furniture with amarinth, Brazilian rosewood and coloured shagreen.

The "Old French Look"

In the United States, some wealthy citizens still favoured opulence (the most extravagant example being San Simeon in California, home of newspaper magnate William Randolph Hearst, built in the 1920s with interiors "collated" from remnants of great European houses) but, on the whole, a plainer, less flamboyant look began to take precedence over the revivalism of the late Victorian era. The "Old French Look," with references to simpler furniture from the Louis XV, Louis XVI and *Directoire* periods, was popularized in America by Elsie de Wolfe (*see* p. 62). Exponents of the new profession of interior decoration prided themselves on understanding all aspects of interior design and principles of proportion and harmony. In "suitable" and well-proportioned rooms, muslin replaced lace curtaining, mirror frames were painted, chairs were upholstered with simple striped fabrics (albeit in satin), and wooden chair frames were treated and lightened. Statuettes held pride of place as singular ornaments, and indoor plants were leafy. Being seen to have "good taste" was all the rage. It was also considered an uncluttering and therefore healthy modern pursuit.

De Wolfe, the country's first professional decorator, began designing in 1897, when she decorated her house in Irving Place near Gramercy Park in New York. Edith Wharton and Ogden Codman's *The Decoration of Houses* (1897, *see* pp. 28–9) inspired her to dismiss the fussy and claustrophobic Victorian interior for a lighter, brighter scheme, incorporating painted furniture and striped walls. The woodwork in the dining room was painted pale gray, the carpet unpatterned. The scheme was admired by New York's leading Beaux-Arts architect, Stanford White, who in 1905 organized a commission for de Wolfe to undertake interior decoration of The Colony Club, a women-only club on Madison Avenue. This was the first public place in America to be designed by a professional interior decorator (it would previously have been treated by an architect or antique dealer), and the results were highly original, with trelliswork inspired by the gardens of Versailles (near Paris) used as an indoor device.

In a single stroke, de Wolfe set a standard and raised awareness of a new chic. Many professional women decorators emerged, thrilled to find an occupation suited to their sex and class. Among those who followed de Wolfe's success in the United States were Nancy McClelland (1876–1959), who ran the decorating department of the store Wanamaker's in New York from 1913 and set up a decorating firm in 1922 specializing in period interiors, as well as writing the definitive book on wallpaper; and Ruby Ross Wood (*see* p. 30), who ghost-wrote articles for de Wolfe in *Ladies' Home Journal* – later interwoven into de Wolfe's book, *The House in Good Taste* (1913). In 1930s Britain, Sibyl Colefax (*see* p. 30) and Syrie Maugham (*see* p. 63) were the leading women decorators, both working mainly on domestic commissions.

The American Institute of Interior Decorators, which became the American Society of Interior Decorators, was established in 1931. Men entered the profession – most, like London-born Terence Harold Robsjohn-Gibbings (1909–73), trained in architecture. Gibbings was brought to New York by antique dealer Charles Duveen and set up a practice on Madison Avenue in 1936, publishing his book *Goodbye Mr Chippendale*, an attack on the cult of antiques, in 1944. His style toed the Moderne line (*see* pp. 60–1).

Although American interiors became more pared-down, they did not on the whole veer toward Modernism. In the United States, Modernism was essentially the vernacular of architects. Decorators who were taken seriously favoured a more romantic look, rooted in tradition. In interior decoration neoclassical style continued and was joined by neo-Baroque (where walls were covered in padded, quilted satin, and sofas and chairs in satin were tufted, stitched, buttoned and piped) and *Directoire*-Modern, which incorporated classic Graeco-Roman shapes and motifs. On both sides of the Atlantic, while decorators like these worked with old forms in refreshingly new ways, there were others who were absorbed in a neoteric world of original thought and aspiration, kindled by a seminal moment in the 20th-century history of the interior: the Paris Exhibition of 1925.

Art Deco

Following the success of the 1900 Paris Universal Exhibition, which validated France's pre-eminence in the creation of Art Nouveau (*see* pp. 159–61), the *Société des Artistes Décorateurs* (founded in 1901) planned, between 1907 and 1912, an exhibition of decorative arts, hoping to improve standards of French design and to challenge exhibitions held by German designers associated with the Deutscher Werkbund (*see* p. 96). It was to take place in 1915 but, because of World War I, was postponed to 1925.

The Paris 1925 *Exposition Internationale des Arts Décoratifs et Industriels Modernes* marked the zenith of Art Deco (the name, used from about

Below: This double-height octagonal room in a house interior designed by David Kleinberg (of David Kleinberg Design Associates, New York) has five walls of windows and hexagonal terracotta floor tiles. The vast table from the 1960s is steel and mahogany, while the armchairs are 1940s French. Narwal tusks form a sculpture. The overall effect is simple elegance in a large and unusual room.

Above: Stephen Ryan (who used to work for David Hicks) designed his own London sitting room based on Syrie Maugham's white-on-white scheme. The medallion chairs (derived from Louis XVI) are white-leather-covered bleached oak, the sofa is in cream damask, and an uplighter appears as a mirrored obelisk. The maquette is by John Kelly, and the portrait after Baldini. A bust of Hera is used as the room's focal point.

1935, was taken from the exhibition title – the symbol of Art Deco became a rising sun). It included work by prominent French designers Emile Jacques Ruhlmann, Pierre Chareau (*see* p. 99) and René Lalique. Swiss artisan Jean Dunand (1877–1942) designed a smoking room for "A French Embassy Abroad," including Cubist-inspired chairs and lacquered walls. Le Corbusier (*see* p. 98) presented his uncompromisingly modern "*Pavilion de l'Esprit Nouveau*" and Josef Hoffmann (*see* p. 95) his Austrian Pavilion, with its hard geometric motifs, at the exhibition, seen as a pivotal moment in architectural history too. One of the most remarkable interiors of the 20th century had its inception after the expo: the Modernist redecoration of the palace of the Maharaja of Indore in India under Eckhart Muthesius (*see* p. 96) from 1930, which was the collaborative effort of many who showed varying styles at the exhibition, including Emile Ruhlmann, Louis Sognot, Eileen Gray, René Herbst, Le Corbusier and Da Silva Bruhns.

Moderne style

In both Britain and the United States, public buildings were at the heart of Art Deco style (including a British look known as "Odeon," following the design of numerous cinemas – two cinemas in this style were opening each week in Britain by 1935). Many public buildings combined Art Deco with Modernism, in a style termed Moderne in America. Oswald P. Milne's lounge at Claridges Hotel in London (from 1930) is a clear example of Art Deco and restrained Modernism with a luxurious flavour, featuring a startling geometrically patterned black-and-ivory carpet by Marion Dorn. Designer Basil Ionides decorated the interior of the Savoy Theatre in London (rebuilt by architects Easton and Robertson in 1928–30) using hues of rust, beige and coral for seating fabric. The audit-orium was covered in silver leaf lacquered in various shades of gold; the hallway of black marble and mirrors supported gold and silver carvings. The smaller Whitehall Theatre, built around the same time by architects E. Stone and Partners, was no less elaborate, and the Cambridge Theatre (also in London), decorated by Serge Chermayeff, while a little more austere, had an auditorium treated with shades of gold. All these interiors had little reference to historical styles and explored a new kind of contemporary decoration characterized by use of strip and neon lighting. If the Depression had not struck, their influence would have been widely felt, but the style (which could be considered a very English combination of Art Deco and Modernism) was quashed before it could filter through to the average home. However, some designers working in this manner in Britain, such as Australian Raymond McGrath (whose hallway for Mansfield Forbes's house in Cambridge was in coloured glass and metal; the staircase featured a lemon-yellow mirror and lavender doors) and Oliver Hill (who used mirrors extensively and was the first to bring sheets of laminated wood into a room with no allusion to period panelling), were widely published and maintained an affluent clientele.

At the 1925 Paris Expo, two nations were notably absent: Germany, for political reasons, and the United States. The Americans declined to take part on the grounds that they had no modern decorative and industrial arts. They had talented architects, such as Frank Lloyd Wright, but, until Eliel Saarinen and the Cranbrook Academy (*see* pp. 162–4), decorative artists were under-represented. However, American delegates turned up in droves to see the exotic materials the Europeans, particularly the French, were mastering and new shapes that were unfolding, including Cubist-inspired geometry.

Minnesota-born Donald Deskey (1894–1989), trained as an architect, attended the expo and was affected by the radical new designs and materials. He brought a modern decorative style to New York from 1926, when he set up a design company with Phillip Vollmar. This gave birth to a distinctly American style known as Streamlined Moderne, which anticipated many designs for Hollywood film sets. It evolved from both Art Deco and the Bauhaus – furniture was low, simple and horizontal, based on fundamental shapes: rectangle, circle and triangle. Lines were sleek and free-form curves featured. Materials included brass, chrome and aluminium (rather than wood); Deskey was the first to use glass-topped tables. He designed, among other buildings, the Radio City Music Hall in New York in 1933, and won prizes at the Paris Universal Exhibition of 1937 and the New York World's Fair in 1939.

In Britain, Betty Joel (1896–1985) set up her furniture and decorating business in 1921, with a factory near Portsmouth on the south coast (producing furniture with a neo-Georgian inflection, mainly in oak and teak) and later a shop in London (boasting 12 room settings at its opening). Her work was mostly commercial, including hotels and boardrooms. In the 1930s she became more Modernistic (inspired by the geometry of Art Deco), but was not a Functionalist. Joel was known for fitted furniture, now considered a precursor of modular schemes, and at the 1935 Royal Academy exhibition "British Art in Industry," she showed a revolving bed.

The late 20th century saw a return to the clean lines coupled with high-level craftsmanship and hand-crafted natural materials found in French 1940s furniture; this was largely a reaction to the consumer-driven 1980s' fashion for sharp, minimal matt-black and chrome, in both homes and offices. New Yorker Raymond Paynter (owner of the London gallery Hemisphere), who was instrumental in the trend in both Britain and America, attributed it partly to the fact that neoclassical, elegant tones could blend with almost any period.

Below: International designer David Collin's apartment in Chelsea, London, evokes the affluent France of the early-to-mid-20th century. The parchment-covered chest is by Jacques Adnet, and the mirror by Line Vautrin. Watercolours by Christian Bérard are hung in frames by Jean-Michel Frank. The table is Swedish.

Elsie de Wolfe

The first professional American decorator, Elsie de Wolfe (1865–1950) had turned 40 by her first commission, in 1905, for The Colony Club on New York's Madison Avenue. There she applied the maxim "simplicity, suitability and proportion." (Previously, working as an actress, she was known less for acting ability than for impeccable Paris couture – *Harper's Bazaar* named her "best-dressed woman of the American stage" in 1900.) Also in 1905, she and her companion and former manager, Elisabeth (Bessie) Marbury, bought the Villa Trianon in Versailles, near Paris, as a showcase for her talent and a base for buying furniture.

De Wolfe (a woman of demure style but not temperament, according to Albert Hadley) personalized the ideas of Ogden Codman and Edith Wharton (*see* pp. 28–9) to form the "Old French Look." Her trademark was decorative simplification. Rooms were clear of clutter and housed well-chosen objects; walls were divided into panels, and colours were tender: pale grays, rose pink, soft blues and ubiquitous white, backdrops for tarnished gilding (later she also made pale-blue "heliotrope" a fashionable hair colour). She was fond of soft floral chintzes, bold stripes, Chinese wallpaper and ornaments such as blackamoors; jardinières and trellises were used indoors. Antiques sat alongside new lucite furniture, leopard-design fabrics adorned cushions, and topiary plants were abundant. Ideas came from 18th-century art and design; her furniture showed Rococo influence. Parquet floors were often evident, as were other French-inspired inflections. Her work combined previous specialist roles such as cabinet-maker and upholsterer, pioneering the profession of interior designer.

As her style matured, de Wolfe made even more sweeping design statements. In 1913 Henry Clay Frick asked her to decorate private apartments at the Frick Mansion in New York. Her book *The House in Good Taste*, serialized in the *Ladies' Home Journal*, was also published in 1913, and her popularity grew. The book almost insisted that Americans improve their homes in the name of patriotism.

In the 1920s and '30s de Wolfe spent time in France, where she decorated homes of expatriate Americans. In New York, she was spurred on by magazine-created rivalries between decorators, until in 1937 her business fell bankrupt. In 1926, at the age of 60, she had married Sir Charles Mendl, a British diplomat in Paris; World War II drove them out of Europe, and in 1940 they moved to Beverly Hills, California, to a house which Elsie decorated with green lacquered walls, massive mirrors and her signature bold stripes. Cecil Beaton described her as a *religieuse*, with fashion her god: "A woman of unquenchable vitality, whose interests were linked with fashion in all its forms, Lady Mendl was so successful she became a living factory of chic."

Below: In the Villa Trianon's pavilion, de Wolfe used striped fabric and elements inspired by 18th-century France. The tree and banquette sofa seen here were later used in California by Michael Taylor.

BIOGRAPHY

1865	Born in New York.
1879–82	Lived in Scotland.
1885	Debutante in London.
1886	Began acting career.
1897–8	Decorated house shared with Elisabeth Marbury in New York.
1905	Designed Colony Club. Bought Villa Trianon.
1913	Decorated Frick Mansion, New York. Published *The House in Good Taste*.
1922	Awarded *Legion d'Honneur* and *Croix de Guerre* for wartime nursing in France.
1926	Married Sir Charles Mendl.
1940	Moved to California.
1950	Died in France.

Syrie Maugham

Syrie Maugham (1879–1955) is known for introducing "pickled" finishes to 18th-century furniture, as well as mirrored glass and a taste for muted tones and toned-down Baroque forms. After a lively youth, she opened a shop in London, called "Syrie," in 1922. This catapulted her to fame as an interior decorator and furniture dealer: customers included actor and playwright Noël Coward, editor Clare Boothe Luce, art collectors Ava and Paul Mellon, actresses Tallulah Bankhead and Mary Pickford, and Mrs Simpson and the Duke of Windsor.

The most talked-about Maugham creation was the interior of her own 17th-century house at 213 King's Road, in London's Chelsea, whose salon she dramatically opened to her artistic friends at midnight in April 1927; it was featured in *Harper's Bazaar* in October 1929. This exposure of her "all-white room" – in fact a tapestry of shades of white, pearl, oyster and ivory – proved good publicity for her decorating business. The white symphony included sofas covered in palest beige satin, off-white-painted Louis XV chairs and a textured carpet by American carpet and textile designer Marion Dorn (who also designed for London's Savoy, Claridges and Berkeley hotels). Many mirrors and indirect, discreet lighting added to the theatricality of the room, often said to have been the origin of the all-white idiom (although this could equally be attributed to a number of other decorators).

Maugham went on to produce many white schemes for clients, including a bedroom in a house by David Adler in 1930 in San Mateo, California. The white craze peaked in 1932, but *Architectural Review* declared it dead by 1934, the year Maugham sold her villa in Le Touquet on France's north coast (decorated to great acclaim in 1926) to concentrate on professional decorating. For the next five years she produced furniture, inspired by 18th-century French "provincial" furniture and identifiable by her signature artificial craquelure or "pickled" finish (although her craftsman was reluctant to show her how he produced it). Pieces were painted different colours, with mouldings highlighted in others: ivory with pale pink, indigo with orange, dark green with white. She departed from her all-white style in favour of blue and then red, then myriads of colour. She was fond of blackamoors, wide neo-Regency stripes, and use of long fringing where a gimp or braid would normally appear on a sofa or chair.

In 1937, Maugham became the London agent for Comtesse Hervé de la Morinière's popular shell ornaments; by 1939 she had sold the contents of her shop to department store Fortnum and Mason and left for New York. Her schemes influenced many decorators (designer Michael Taylor [*see* pp. 168–71] referred to her "look" in his schemes in California in the 1970s) and filtered through to Hollywood movie-set design. Her fame was such that Evelyn Waugh parodied her as Mrs Beaver in his novel *A Handful of Dust*, and Beverly Nichols as the Countess of Westbourne in *For Adults Only*.

BIOGRAPHY

1879	Born Gwendoline Maude Syrie Barnardo, daughter of founder of homes for destitute children, in London.
1917	Second marriage, to playwright/novelist Somerset Maugham.
1922	Opened first shop, on Baker Street, London.
1926–7	Opened shops in New York and Chicago.
1927–37	Heyday as decorator, working on both sides of the Atlantic.
1929	Divorced.
1938–9	Worked on Wilsford Manor, Wiltshire, with artist Stephen Tennant.
1939–44	Lived in New York.
1955	Died.

Above: Maugham's all-white room (in fact, the sofa is oyster satin) in Chelsea, London, was created in 1927 (and photographed in 1929). The textured carpet is by Marion Dorn.

Emile Ruhlmann

BIOGRAPHY

1879 Born in Paris.
1907 Took over father's decorating business.
1911 Patronized by architect Charles Plumet. Showed wallpapers at *Salon des Artistes Décorateurs.*
1913 Showed dining room at *Salon d'Automne.*
1919 Established new business, became an *ensemblier.*
1925 Career peaked at Paris Exposition.
1926 Designed interior for the Elysée Palace.
1927 Exhibited in Madrid and Milan.
1930 Designed "*Soleil*" bed in rosewood as a commission for Jean Renouardt.
1932 Designed French Embassy in Tokyo.
1933 Died.

The leading designer and decorator in France between 1918 and 1926, Emile Jacques Ruhlmann (1879–1933) worked in an elegantly pared-down 1760s neoclassical idiom from his first showing of luxury furniture in a dining room at the *Salon d'Automne* in 1913 until the late 1920s; his later work was more Modernistic, using chromium-plated steel, silver and black lacquer (as in the palace of the Maharaja of Indore, *see* p. 60). He is credited with taking Art Deco to opulent extremes, using rare materials such as inlaid ivory, ebony, amboyna, lizard skin, shagreen (sharkskin) and tortoiseshell. Soft woods were also used. Ruhlmann's furniture was never in industrial production and a year would elapse from placement of an order to production of a hand-crafted piece; from 1928 pieces were issued with serial number, certificate of authentication and signature. Many forms were drawn from features associated with *Empire* style (*see* p. 12), including drum-shaped tables and fluted legs with feet covered in ivory tips called *sabots*. Gilt-metal finishes to wood and tubular, upholstered cushions in rich fabrics and colours were characteristic of his style. These historical references blended with geometric Cubist forms in a quest for "harmony."

Around 1901, Ruhlmann joined his father (a prosperous house decorator from Alsace) in his Paris wallpaper and painting firm, where he learned to work with sumptuous materials. On his father's death, in 1907, he took over the firm. The same year, he married, and designed his own home in a style set to evolve into one of the most distinctive of the interwar period.

After World War I, he built up a large furniture workshop, Etablissements Ruhlmann et Laurent, also designing carpets, textiles and fittings, and became an *ensemblier* with painter and decorator Pierre Laurent. Ruhlmann's talent was visualizing and sketching (he employed 16 draftsmen to translate his sketches, and paid all staff and skilled workmen well). The Depression had little impact on his career: wealthy private clients remained faithful, as did the French government, which had him design its embassies – showcases for the best French design and decoration (as were oceanliners; Ruhlmann did the tea room of the *Île de France*).

His greatest triumph was his rooms for the 1925 Paris Exposition, "*Hôtel du Collectionneur*," which epitomized Art Deco (classically inspired entablature encircled the main room at ceiling height; other rooms featured patterned wallpapers and carpets, grand but streamlined chandeliers, and wall-panels designed by Jean Dupas). Ruhlmann's interior for the scent company Yardley's store in London, designed with Reco Capey, was changed after World War II, but surviving elements were given to the Brighton Museum to mark Yardley's 200th anniversary. Ruhlmann died aged 54, still enjoying accolades for his uncompromising work.

Right: Ruhlmann's furniture was often based on 18th-century *gondole* (gondola) type. His hand-crafted luxury furnishings indicated French emphasis on quality. At the Paris 1925 expo, his "*Hôtel du Collectionneur*" ("House of a Collector") was considered one of the great Art Deco achievements.

Jean-Michel Frank

Modernist, Surrealist and occasional avant-gardist, Jean-Michel Frank (born in Paris in 1895) was one of the most influential and emulated figures in design in the late 20th century, and a true innovator (the first to use white-leaded wood in the 1920s). As Stephen Sills, of Sills Huniford (*see* pp. 82–5), explains, "He was the first person who understood spirituality in decoration. He understood the greatest decoration of the past – the entire history from ancient Egyptian to Ming to Louis XVI – and reinvented it in a modern sensibility of proportions and rare-quality woods and materials. That made him the greatest decorator of the 20th century. It is almost banal now to follow J.-M. Frank, but he was the Picasso of decoration."

However, Frank had a tragic life. In 1915 his two brothers were killed in World War I. His father committed suicide soon after, and his mother died in an asylum, where she had lived for several years. He was also the great-uncle of wartime diarist Anne Frank. His own death was by suicide (like a number of other refugee German-Jewish artists), at the age of 46, when, desperate and lovesick, he jumped from the St Regis Hotel in New York.

Frank's most productive period was the 1930s, when he collaborated with Parisian decorator Adolphe Chanaux. (Born in 1887, Chanaux studied at the *Ecole des Beaux-Arts* before working for André Groult, Emile Jacques Ruhlmann [*see* p. 64] – whom Frank also worked for – and cabinet-maker Pelletier.) After Chanaux decorated Frank's apartment, they set up shop together at 140 rue du Faubourg St Honoré. Renowned for simple but expensively elegant interiors, Frank supplied quality furniture with emphasis on rare materials (some proscribed) to leading American decorators Elsie de Wolfe (*see* p. 62), Syrie Maugham (*see* p. 63), Frances Elkins and Eleanor Brown (*see* p. 33). The shop also sold pieces designed with Emilio Terry, Diego and Alberto Giacometti, Christian Bérard and Salvador Dali (Dali's "Mae West Lips" sofa appeared in a Paris cinema-cum-ballroom designed by Frank for Baron Roland de l'Espée in 1936). Occasionally, Frank lectured too, at Parsons School of Design in Paris.

His designs, usually rectilinear, were partly inspired by Le Corbusier (*see* p. 98) and Robert Mallet-Stevens (*see* p. 99). Mallet-Stevens helped him acquire his best-known commission, the villa of Vicomte and Vicomtesse de Noailles in Hyères in the south of France. A key design of the century was his Hôtel Bischoffsheim residence in Paris, also for the Noailles, where furniture was in Macassar ebony, walls were covered in beige vellum, sofas in bleached leather, and screens in shagreen, leather and lacquer. His interior for Elsa Schiaparelli in the mid-1930s was a melange of brightly coloured chintzes and black. After decorating Nelson Rockefeller's apartment in New York (1937), Frank wanted to settle in America; Eleanor Brown is said to have provided the backing. Today, just one project by Jean-Michel Frank remains intact: a three-room apartment in a 16th-century palazzo near Rome.

BIOGRAPHY

1895	Born in Paris.
1904	Started school: Lycée Janson de Sailly, Paris.
1911	Started law school.
1920–5	Travelled widely.
1920s	Met exotic Chilean Eugenia Errazuriz; influenced by her skill in mixing provincial Louis XVI furniture with modern lighting.
1924–33	Designed the Noailles' villa in Hyères, France.
1929	Designed Hôtel Bischoffsheim residence, Paris.
1932	Opened shop with Adolphe Chanaux.
1939–40	Left for South America, then USA.
1941	Committed suicide.

Left: In the Modernist-inspired Templeton-Crocker apartment in San Francisco (1937), Frank used mirrored wall-panels, glass ramps, and metal and lacquered panels. The convertible armchair, shown here in the drawing room, becomes a deck chair or flat bench; it was produced in oak that had been blackened and then cerused (white-leaded), and has wool trimmings.

Frédéric Méchiche

"I am interested in everything, perhaps because very early on I met people from all origins, all walks of life, and was lucky enough to witness some splendid collections."

Paris-based designer Frédéric Méchiche is a self-confessed perfectionist who likes to do everything himself, from conceptualizing through to overseeing final details. He does not hesitate to use "epoch" furniture with primitive works of art or stringently contemporary pieces.

Méchiche spent his childhood in Algeria and Switzerland, the son of a doctor "with a passion for architecture and decoration, and for each and every period of antiquity right up to the current day."

Left: Four tables of his own design, granite-topped with matt-painted metal supports, form the dining arrangement in Méchiche's Paris apartment. The room, with white-painted late-18th-century *boiserie*, contains 19th-century *Restauration* chairs signed Janselme, a Louis XVI mirror, a 1960s sculpture and Danish 1950s glass. The 1982 portrait of Gill Chapman is by Mapplethorpe.

Having shown an interest in architecture from the age of ten, Frédéric studied interior architecture at the *Ecole Camondo* in Paris (the faculty was part of the *Union Centrale des Arts Décoratifs*). Even as a student he received prestigious private commissions; more recent projects have included a penthouse in Caracas (in Venezuela), a castle in England, a London townhouse, a New York apartment, a house in Hong Kong and a yacht in Greece. In France, Méchiche masterminds Parisian apartments as well as country houses and homes on the Côte d'Azur, and has applied his creativity to Joël Robuchon's restaurant The Astor and Dokhans at the Trocadéro. His Paris showroom displays furniture designs as subtle yet quietly fashionable as Méchiche is himself.

Yves Gastou

"I just want to bear witness to the savoir-faire of the French design community after the Second World War, and to keep an eye on the future, on quality contemporary design."

Paris gallery owner Yves Gastou, a specialist in 20th-century furniture and artifacts, has helped bring many unsung designers of the mid-20th century to public attention, especially via his gallery on rue Bonaparte on Paris's Left Bank. While he has also promoted recent work, his passion is for French designers of the 1940s – among them master ironworker Gilbert Poillerat, painter and textile artist Christian Bérard, and furniture-makers Marc du Plantier, Jean Royère, Jean-Michel Frank (*see* p. 65), Jacques Adnet and André Arbus. "It is more interesting to rediscover the quality craftsmanship of Arbus or du Plantier than collect pieces of great skill and value which everyone knows already," he says. "What I like about the 1940s is the collaborative efforts. They worked together, often on a single piece." In 1996, Gastou was invited to participate in the 18th prestigious *Biennale Internationale des Antiquaires* in Paris. This was the first time French decorative arts of the 1940s had been deemed of high enough quality to be showcased alongside styles from previous centuries.

Gastou has also promoted more recent and avant-garde designers, such as André Dubreuil, Ettore Sottsass (*see* pp. 172–7), Alessandro Mendini

Left: In a client's Paris apartment, sofas and chairs are by André Arbus. A bronze statuette of Mowgli from *The Jungle Book* sits on a black-lacquered and gilt-bronze table by Jacques Adnet. The bronze-and-marble table is by Gilbert Poillerat, the carpet by Jacques Despierre. An original Raymond Delamarre plaster model of Mowgli hangs above the stone staircase.

and Ron Arad (*see* p. 165) in his gallery. In 1994, he reintroduced the neoclassically inspired sculpture of Raymond Delamarre (creator of the imposing figures at the Palais de Chaillot in Paris), and he was the first in France to show the surrealistic furniture of Tokyo designer Shiro Kuramata. "My gallery is the opposite to a museum," he says, in the French equivalent of a Southern drawl.

Born in 1948, Gastou left school at 15 for an apprenticeship with an antique dealer and gallery owner who specialized in the 18th and 19th centuries, based in Carcassonne in the south of France. There he became familiar not only with the strict lines of early-19th-century *Empire* style but also with the Art Nouveau work of Emile Gallé, Hector Guimard and others on the cusp of the 20th century. In 1971 he opened his own gallery dedicated to Art Nouveau and Art Deco. "I was interested in these two styles opposed to prevalent bourgeois styles. I embrace furniture and objects of beauty and quality which other people have been indifferent to. In the beginning I only helped put these things on the map in a provincial way – much of the success of designers I promoted was down to the dealers I supplied in the cities and some forward-thinking collectors."

Leaving Carcassonne for Toulouse, Gastou became interested in contemporary work. In 1981 he went with his friend, collector Jean Galvani, to the Milan Fair, where they met Sottsass, Mendini and Andrea Branzi. "I realized pieces of the 1980s were antiques of the future. We should stop living retro and give young designers a chance to account for the end of this century. I have been a risk-taker and relied on my eye to find those who will be celebrated tomorrow. I present only those I like and believe in." On a quest for 1980s pieces, Gastou stumbled across works by designer, architect and photographer Carlo Mollino and recognized their value. He started to collect and sell pieces from the 1950s, '60s and '70s too, including glassware by Pablo Picasso and Jean Arp and a lamp signed Jean Cocteau. Part antiquarian, part dealer, Gastou took a stall at the weekend Paris fleamarket at Clignancourt for a few years in the early 1980s.

In 1986 he and his wife, Françoise, moved to Paris permanently, opening the gallery on rue Bonaparte (its granite front designed by Sottsass). Françoise, who gave up law to assist in the Toulouse gallery, works at her husband's side. Their home, a Paris boulevard apartment, pays homage to the 1940s artists and designers Gastou has given exposure to. Although primarily a gallery owner, he has furnished apartments for client-friends, his work embodying the spirit of mid-century France.

Above left: A stone statue from classical antiquity stands in front of an iron balustrade by André Dubreuil and a 15th-century French tapestry. The glass-and-forged-iron light fitting is by Eric Schmitt. The mahogany doors are embellished with neoclassical motifs. **Right:** In this room the carpet is early-19th-century Aubusson. Classical embellishments on the French daybed frame include stylized foliage motifs, echoed in the fireplace carvings.

Albert Hadley

"Such innovations as lacquered walls, modern lighting, even classic Oriental tables bound in raffia and dipped in enamel paint were included in my design vocabulary. We work with artists and artisans to create objects of classical inspiration but pure 20th-century spirit."

One of the 20th century's pre-eminent American interior designers, Albert Hadley worked in partnership with Mrs Henry "Sister" Parish (*see* pp. 40–3). He achieved recognition for his attention to architecture and the arrangement of art and furniture in a well-proportioned space; his rooms are always appropriate, perfectly tailored and supremely detailed. Hadley's skills derive in part from his education at the leading Parsons School of Design in New York under some of the most meticulous and far-seeing design experts of the mid-century, a debt he recognizes with gratitude. Prime among these was Van Day Truex (later design director at Tiffany), who was then president of Parsons. Day Truex had been trained in design by both William Odom and the New York school's founder, Frank Alvar Parsons, a contemporary of Edith Wharton and Ogden Codman (*see* pp. 28–9). Apart from this mainly American influence, Hadley benefited from Day Truex's passion for the elegance of French designers of the time and his keenness to advance the cause of Modernism. Day Truex knew Jean-Michel Frank (*see* p. 65) from the days when he headed the Paris branch of Parsons, and adopted and popularized

Left: Classic upholstered furniture, Hepplewhite chairs and Regency benches furnish a pale-gray New York salon, which has been saved from fresh paint since 1969 – a triumph, according to Albert Hadley. The pilasters and dentil cornice (crown molding) were salvaged from a historical building nearby.

Frank's designs and philosophies, which later translated into Hadley's work. Hadley's use of unexpected textures, animal-skin rugs, stylized furniture, exotic accessories and subtly lit rooms, where light and shadow enhance architectural wonder, can all be seen to have drawn from the mood of the 1940s.

Albert Hadley was born in 1920 in Springfield, near Nashville, Tennessee, where his father's company specialized in farm tools and buggies, and grew up in comfortable surroundings (although not nearly as splendid as the environment Parish, his future partner, was born to). The young Hadley had an inquiring and logical mind, a good visual imagination and an inherent ability to know what would work practically – he even threatened to leave home unless his parents reversed the approach of the driveway to their house. He studied art and design at Peabody College, Nashville, with the aim of becoming an architect, until he realized he had no aptitude for mathematics.

He then went on to train with A. Herbert Rogers, a local decorator ("the best in the South"), who influenced the young Hadley with his French-inflected house and its mansard roof, Versailles parquet, and Chippendale chairs covered in white leather tacked in place with antique silver nails. Rogers also introduced Hadley to the possibilities of silver-leaf paper as a wall covering – which creates a soft, reflective effect, like iridescent rectangular patches of fish scales – now considered a signature of a Hadley interior.

Another influence came by way of the magazines *House & Garden*, *House Beautiful* and *Vogue*, with their coverage of the style-conscious of the day: Elsie de Wolfe (*see* p. 62), whose scalloped lucite chair with leopard-print seat was a particular benchmark of the century for Hadley; Syrie Maugham (*see* p. 63), especially her all-white drawing room in King's Road, London; Dorothy Draper (*see* p. 130) with her confectionery Baroque plasterwork for Essex House, New York; Sibyl Colefax (*see* p. 30) and her palm-based plaster tables; and the innovations of William Pahlmann (*see* p. 129). Hadley saw the latter as "the modern Merlin: the top-flight decorator for Lord and Taylor," whose room sets could only be described as prescient: "I remember sand on the floor of a Pahlmann scheme, there was a single chair and a piece of blue glass – and this was the 1940s."

After two years as Rogers's assistant at the Period Furniture Company in Nashville, Hadley hoped to move to New York, but war came and he was drafted into the US Army and stationed in England. This proved advantageous in opening up new opportunities: at Rainbow Corner, the headquarters for US servicemen in Piccadilly, London, where Hadley spent his day of leave each week, he met a volunteer, Adele Astaire, Lady Cavendish

Above left: This study was created by Hadley for the Kips Bay show house in the Andrew Carnegie Mansion, Manhattan (1973). He found the shagreen desk and Jean-Michel Frank furniture in a storage room in the house, and restored wood panels originally by Louis Comfort Tiffany. **Right:** Detail of this New Jersey salon shows its simple scheme, with bare parquet flooring and fabrics kept to ivory cotton, silks and subtle chintzes.

(Fred Astaire's sister). She introduced him to Constance Spry (a well-known taste-maker and genius at flower arrangement) and Emma Shields (who owned a shop dedicated to white). Exposed to others' creativity, he wanted to continue in similar vein.

Following the war, he returned to Nashville, then went to New York. In 1947 he approached the doyenne of professional American interior design, Eleanor Brown (*see* p. 33) of McMillen Inc, about a position, but all McMillen employees had to be formally trained (almost exclusively at Parsons), Brown being a stickler for education in architectural elements, proportion and detail, if not architecture itself. Having been rejected because he had not been to Parsons, Hadley was keen to find out what the school had to offer.

Above: In a Hadley apartment in a 1930s Chicago building for the late Alan Daskal, the carpet is by Edward Fields Carpets and curtains (over bamboo blinds) by Mrs Tillet. The chandelier is early American *tôle*. Cushions are fur and silk velvet; artifacts include an albino tortoiseshell. **Right:** A North Carolina penthouse has neoclassical chairs and trompe-l'oeil walls painted white over green. Indian wedding mirrors open to reveal a television.

He initially enrolled for a six-week summer course at Parsons, but was offered a scholarship and stayed to finish the three-year programme, graduating in 1949. He then taught there for five years before setting up on his own on East 57th Street, New York, in 1954. Eleanor Brown finally approached him about a position with McMillen Inc in 1957.

By 1962 Hadley had been instrumental in the success of many projects at McMillen (including the sensitive restoration of Rosedown Plantation, Louisiana, a delightful project for him as a Southerner), but was feeling a little restless. His mentor Van Day Truex suggested he approach Sister Parish (*see* p. 40–3), who had recently asked Day Truex if he knew of "some young man" who could absorb some of the responsibility at her office. At the time, Parish was working on the presidential suites of the White House in Washington, DC, for President and Mrs Kennedy, and had a worldwide reputation for her interiors for the privileged and wealthy. Hadley was in his forties, ten years Parish's junior. He joined Parish's firm in 1963, and went into partnership with her in 1964.

Hadley and Parish developed one of the most influential interior-design firms of the century, with a credo that a room must be unmodish, practical and appropriate. Their styles were almost polar opposites – "If, early in our collaboration, Sis had heard of Modernism, it did not interest her at all. I was the disciple." – yet they were well matched in attitudes to quality, comfort and professionalism. Hadley's contributions to Parish-Hadley Associates have included a redesign of the Nelson Rockefeller apartment on Fifth Avenue, New York, first done by Jean-Michel Frank (*see* p. 65) in 1937, with Christian Bérard and Alberto Giacometti (it was Hadley who recognized the need to preserve classic 20th-century interiors). Since Parish's death in 1994, Hadley continues to direct the 25-strong firm, whose alumni are plotting the way forward for interior design in the United States and elsewhere.

John Saladino

"I don't regard interior design as an applied art, but as a fine art. We look upon the interior as participating in art; it's art that you live in rather than art that you look at."

John F. Saladino, born in Kansas City, Missouri, in 1939, is the son of a doctor who emigrated from Italy in 1923. "Having parents of European origin brought a lot to bear on my present sensibility. We are not born in a vacuum." Love of history – particularly Italian, from the Villa of Mysteries in Pompeii through to Palladio – permeates his work.

A graduate of Notre Dame University and Yale School of Art and Architecture (where he studied painting; he describes his interiors as "walk-in paintings"), Saladino worked in Rome in the late 1960s with architect Piero Sartogo before moving to New York. There he opened his own design practice. "It was painful being a painter. I wasn't married, I was living in New York, which is a technological society. Everyone would go off to work in the morning but me. I wanted to get out and participate." John F. Saladino Inc was founded in 1972 and is now a design company with a staff of 25 (six of them architects), whose projects range from apartment renovations to 250,000sq ft (23,000sq m) office developments. Saladino himself has a passion for preserving the old – he is on the board of directors of the Save Venice movement – and takes on restoration of many buildings.

Left: It took John Saladino eight years to restore his Palladian-style mansion, Robin Hill. The drawing room has a Grinling Gibbons fireplace, Queen Anne chairs and cotton-covered, high-backed modern sofas. There is a 19th-century Turkish rug over parquet flooring and a North African antique chest that serves as a coffee table.

In 1986 he started a furniture company, making comfortable pieces with simple, geometric forms. Collections – for the Dunbar furniture company, Bloomingdales store and, later, Baker, Knapp and Tubbs furniture companies – have won him four prestigious Daphne awards for furniture design. He has also earned numerous *Interior Design* magazine awards and has been on the boards of Formica, Parsons School of Design and Steuben Glass.

In most work, he aims to create "emotional experiences – moments of transcendence;" the link between his projects is romance. "My intention is to create a new reality so emotional that you feel you have entered a special place – what do you do to make a space magic?" A master of scale, he has a knack for making diminutive rooms seem imposing (borrowing architectural features from antiquity to exaggerate dimensions) or creating charming enclaves with tricks of colour and scale.

A technique he invented, now considered an emblem of Saladino style, is "scratch-coat plaster," whereby portions of walls are faded using brown-coat plaster mixed with stone dust, along with a special ingredient – coffee grounds. As the mixture dries, a texture resembling the walls of a crumbling Venetian palazzo appears: "For me a wall sometimes functions like 'fluctuating figure ground,' a concept you find in painting." Another way he artificially decays a room is to take a rag and "ruin" hand-painted murals. "I set up a discipline and when I think it is becoming too perfect, I wreck it." Transition from outdoor to indoor is eased by using exterior materials in entrance halls: "I don't like being hurled into someone's living room – it's so absolutely American to open the front door and find oneself right in the middle of a conversation."

He has a simple formula for fabric: large pieces of upholstery should match the walls or the floor, so that objects, people and even flowers are the focus. Colour is important – the background palette is often in muted tones (but rarely pure white): stone colours, silvers and grays, golds and delicate gray-greens, with interruptions of distressed reds and blues, to delicate and harmonious effect. There is greater colour variety in a Saladino room than first appears. "You have to concern yourself not only with a colour but with the implications as it changes through day or night, or location." He remembers a class taught by Josef Albers at Yale: "He pointed out that Coca-Cola produces bottle tops in two shades of red: a cool red in the south and a warm red in the north. He asked students to bring to class a square of the most intense red they could find. When 30 people put their squares together, some appeared pink, some brown. No two people see one colour the same way."

Saladino enjoys juxtaposition of weathered surfaces with sleek and modern. "Half of me likes the precision and skill that goes into the highly technical 20th-century environment; the other half likes to break all rules and use wood that is hand-planed." He continues to mix old with new, devising solutions to the demands of modern living.

Above: Arched corridors lead in four directions from the central hallway of Saladino's house, Robin Hill, designed in 1927 by Charles Everitt.
Right: A bedroom at the Palladian-style house. Situated in Connecticut's Berkshire mountains, it has six acres of formal garden and 20 acres of woodland. The property had been closed for 20 years, and was in need of complete renovation, when Saladino and his late wife bought it.

Sills and Huniford

"What we truly want to do is not to import Europe, but to draw upon Europe, as Elsie de Wolfe did, and make it American. That is what is original, and what makes for great decorating."

Interior designers Stephen Sills and James Huniford formed their New York company, Sills Huniford Associates, in 1984, with the aim of using furnishings from the 17th century through to the 20th to create refined and sensitive environments that meet all the needs of modern living. Stephen and Ford (as they are affectionately known) find inspiration in 17th- and 18th-century European furniture, Old Master paintings and, particularly, Italian, French and English architecture; it is their keen sense of structure and architecture that lends their decorating schemes so much substance. "There is probably not an ugly room in France," Sills explains in his lilting voice (he grew up in southern Oklahoma). "In America you have to create the room that in Europe already exists. You so rarely find here the architectural features or decorative elements that are so important to the success of any room. That is why I really respect the Ogden Codman, Edith Wharton sensibility."

The pair's depth of knowledge (particularly their grasp of the historical interior) and the quality of their work have led some forward-thinking and aesthetically sophisticated clients to commission interiors, including Mr and Mrs

Left: A bedroom by Sills and Huniford features an unusual gilt Louis XVI "tester" bed (canopies rarely appeared on Louis XVI beds), above which hangs a 19th-century pastel drawing of an Arab. At the back of the room, a 19th-century architect's table supports a Roman bust. The glass light fixture hanging above it is Viennese.

Stephen Swid, Anna Wintour (Editor-in-Chief of American *Vogue*), fashion designer Vera Wang, rock star Tina Turner, Samantha Bass, mountain-and-camping-wear company North Face's Jim and Betsy Fifield, and the Newhouse family. "Our work develops out of a mutual passion, one shared by us and our clients, who are interested in doing something unusual and creative. Nan Swid hired us to design her office, which used to be Billy Baldwin's residence. We learned as much from her modest sensibility, which she had used so successfully in commissioning architects to create household objects for her firm, Swid Powell, as she did from us in terms of working with antique furniture and unusual objects. We have this nature of relationship with many clients," says Huniford.

Sills trained at design school at North Texas University. There he learned the basics of architectural drafting, design and textiles, although he also wanted to be an artist: "I took art classes and worshipped all the usual suspects – Picasso and Matisse – and I painted. I was always interested in interiors but I didn't have access to great rooms, so I scoured magazines all my teenage life. I saw Billy Baldwin's work and it seemed very glamorous to me, this American man who pared down decoration and made it so crisp and clean – timeless and without a tricky edge. Then I embraced the world of exotic interior design. I learned about Cecil Beaton and read articles in *Architectural Digest* filled with fantasy, which had an impact upon my imagination. I made all this a constant study from an early age."

Huniford grew up in Syracuse, New York, and always had a keen eye. "Ford is brilliant at space planning, the architectural side, and is also wonderful at understanding the clients' needs," says Sills. Both travelled in Europe, where they were exposed to the real thing. "That triggered my imagination and put down some kind of foundation," he adds. Ford continues: "15 years ago we had just one or two clients and worked from a one-room apartment on 83rd Street. Then *World of Interiors* did an eight-page story about us and we were featured in *House & Garden*. The phone started ringing and we were launched."

Today, the firm's signature elements include monochromatic colour schemes; the use of rare materials such as parchment, shagreen (sharkskin), honed stones, limed oak and tooled leather; and an emphasis on functionality combined with grace. Sills and Huniford themselves share two very different homes: a serene house on 12 acres of grounds in Bedford, upstate New York, and a compact gem of a 15th-floor Manhattan penthouse, with just three rooms. They cite strong contemporary art influences – their own art collection includes works ranging from Joan Miró to Man Ray – and they believe, as Sills points out, "Understanding the object is the most important part of decorating – the form and what you are looking at. It really is all about objects, and space, isn't it?"

Above: In this apartment, an 18th-century map of a French farm hangs over an English Sheraton table. A console in the hallway is made from glass blocks. **Right:** Sills and Huniford's home in New York state features a painting by Cy Twombly, a *Directoire* sphinx table and 18th-century English twig candle stands. A pair of Louis XVI ammunition cabinets stand by the sofa; the globe was Rudolf Nureyev's. The limestone floor is 18th-century French.

Sills and Huniford's drawing room, in their Manhattan prewar penthouse, combines Modernism and classicism, with a neutral background for remarkable objects and prestige furniture. A 1920s tapestry is by Ernest Boiceau (for Tate and Hall). The sample board (*right*) shows typical Sills and Huniford elements.

Fabric

The drapes, in taupe wool **(1)**, provide a good backdrop for this multi-textured scheme. The sofa on the left is covered in "Collotweed" viscose-and-linen by Pierre Frey in a flesh colour **(2)**. Strie cotton-and-linen velvet by Clarence House **(3)** covers the buttonback banquette on the right. A pair of shagreen cubic benches by Jean-Michel Frank are covered in silk-velvet **(4)**. Pillows are covered in celadon velvet and mustard felt **(5)**. A made-to-order rough-woven satin from Donghia **(6)** covers a rare Jean-Michel Frank shagreen *recamier.*

Floor covering

Hand-woven Congolin floor matting in cotton and raffia **(7)** is from the south of France.

Furniture

The rosewood table is by Eugène Printz, and the leather club chair by Jean-Michel Frank.

Decorative additions

The plaster dado was inspired by a Hellenistic Greek temple. Alabaster lamps are by Jean-Michel Frank, with their original shades. The painting above the banquette, by Christian Bérard, was previously owned by Christian Dior. A large bronze sculpture by Jean Arp entitled "*Coup Chimérique*" (1947) is the scheme's grandest gesture.

Design signatures

Stephen Sills and James Huniford prefer to start with the fundamentals of structure. "This room had nice high ceilings but was architecturally very uninteresting, so we created a heavy, tall crown moulding in plaster at the top and made the walls into linear strips which, when divided, set up a grid for the background of the room, giving the walls an architectural quality." The powdery blue-gray walls were lined with linen, which was stencilled with dark Moorish-type motifs and then sealed with a semi-transparent glaze, applied dozens of times, to create a softening patina.

Emphasis on proportions

"In this room, we lifted the doors up high and elevated the room – which is why the rectilinear forms work. They are, in turn, offset by the curves of some of the art." Here, this includes the fluid forms of a painting by Christian Bérard and a bronze by Jean Arp. An 18th-century Italian mirror with original glass draws the eye to the ceiling, exaggerating the room's size.

Drawing from history

Sills and Huniford aim to draw their creations from classicism as much as from Modernism. Their 1940s pieces, for instance, are inspired mainly by the 18th century.

Awareness of light

All windows were changed from sliding glass doors to specially made windows that let in as much light as possible yet retained a grid design in keeping with the general shape of the room.

Focus on texture

They believe in using both rough and luxuriant fabrics, in complementary tones. The variety of texture works with the furniture fabrics to give the room a rich, warm background.

Jonathan Reed

"Texture is far more important than colour – the worked stone with the unworked stone, the shiny and the matt, the velvet with the silk. I love to see the touch of the hand when things are made."

British designer Jonathan Reed is driven by a love of the natural world, of fine artifacts (from ancient to 20th-century pieces) and of scientific precision – characteristics fundamental to the work of his interior-design company. In tones as calming as his interiors, he attributes much of his taste to growing up in the north of England. "Being a Yorkshireman is important to my approach: pragmatic, practical and straightforward. You can't fail to be impressed by things that surround you when you are young – the slate, the dry-stone walls, the look of the rain beating the stone, it is all etched on my mind. Organic material is part of what I take as my natural language."

Born in 1964, Reed's talent for science (he still likes chemistry) led him to study physiology at university in London. At the same time, he spent his weekends buying furniture and artifacts in Yorkshire to sell at London streetmarkets; soon he found Japanese clients to buy for and gave up his studies.

A job as head of development for the menswear company Hackett was followed by a spell at Ralph Lauren, where he was a designer for the new Polo stores during their expansion into Europe. At Ralph Lauren he met Ann Boyd, with whom he

Left: Designer Anna Jagdfelds, preoccupied with the design of her own store in East Berlin, turned to Reed to design her impeccable apartment in the same building (by architect I. M. Pei). Sliding vellum panels screen the windows; in front is a table by André Arbus, a silver-plated lamp and two Reed chairs upholstered in Marquis fabric by Sahco Hesslein.

went on to establish a London design company that ran for several years. One early commission was the apartment of the Byblos fashion-design team. He has created offices and homes for a range of illustrious clients, including houses for the Rothschild family and an office for Susan Crewe, Editor-in-Chief of British *House & Garden*. He also has his eye on larger projects: "I'd like to do a hotel."

In his own company, Reed Design, set up in 1997, Reed exercises his passion for creating interior elements, furniture and objects from rare and refined but natural materials: parchment; honed, polished and battered stone; and wood that has been fumed, wire-brushed, bleached, sandblasted and scrubbed. He recognizes what is worth preserving, and is committed to detail. His rooms are deeply textured (combining vellum, lacquer, slate, leather, hand-forged iron and wenge wood) and bare but luxurious, reflecting the contemporary desire to avoid excess but live in comfort. "The trend of the 1990s has been to strip everything out, to be bare and minimal. It will be seen as the style of the decade, but eventually we'll transcend it: people will begin to crave luxury."

From the salubrious and vast showroom in London's Sydney Street, the eight-person design team focus on producing quality interiors, with no room for compromise. "First we approach the architecture, the space. I like things precisely engineered but not over-engineered. We start from the materials: the way they join, function and are contrasted. In the end we become obsessed about toning in plugs so you don't see them in a wall.... Our colour envelope is neutral at the moment – taupe, dark brown, beige and black – but we inject sharp contrasts such as acid green and yellow."

Reed's signature "Beehive" range of furniture (currently in fumed oak) exhibits an enticing symmetry and simplicity. His slate tables border on the organic and could be at home in a scheme by Californian Michael Taylor (*see* pp. 168–71). But there is no set Reed look: "Having a stock style is no challenge, although it is easier because the public commit to you if they know what you're going to give them. The worst thing with starting each project from scratch is you never know if you are going to work again, whether people will like what you do. It is odd what makes people like things."

Above left: In Jagdfelds's bedroom, Reed designed a fumed-oak and woven-tape screen as a bedhead; the bed covering is soft denim, lined with sable. **Above:** A polished-steel 19th-century bath on a marble slab is separated from the shower by a ribbed stone wall. **Right:** A vellum banquette by Jean-Michel Frank stands in front of tobacco-leaf lacquer cabinets and a bleached-oak frieze, both designed and made by Reed.

Cecil Beaton
TREASURES OF THE FORBIDDEN CITY

CONTEMPORARY

The Modern movement began after World War I, when an intellectual acceleration took place in the arts, with Constructivism in Russia, Cubism in France and De Stijl in Holland. Artists painted in an architectural manner (some even designed furniture) and architects built in a painterly way; Le Corbusier was in fact a painter before he was an architect. Although Modern-movement protagonists shared many ideas with Arts and Crafts or Art Nouveau, they differed in that they chose to design furniture that could be mass-produced.

Above: The German Pavilion for the 1929 Barcelona Exhibition, with its "Barcelona" chairs and ottomans, was built by Ludwig Mies van der Rohe. Costly materials were used; their surfaces were left undecorated so that they could be fully appreciated.

Previous pages: Christian Liaigre rejuvenated this extraordinary Mallet-Stevens house – the Villa Martel, owned by art collector Karsten Greve – restoring many original features and redesigning others. The dressing table and chairs in sycamore and metal are authentic by Mallet-Stevens; the standard lamp is by Giacometti. The simple 1932 sculpture on the table by Alexander Calder is entitled "Kiki's Nose."

The Modern movement's exponents embraced technology and sought to explore new materials. One difference between the 19th and 20th centuries as far as a home was concerned, according to the Modernists, was that between hand and machine. Aesthetically things were different too. In the 19th century, structure was concealed, in both architecture and furniture, whereas in the 20th, it was emphasized. The functionalism of much furniture designed between the world wars suits needs and tastes today. For example, the "Barcelona" chair by Ludwig Mies van der Rohe (*see* p. 98) – so called because it was designed for the German Pavilion at the Barcelona International Exhibition in 1929 – is still in production (with matching ottoman and table) and widely appreciated for its simple curved-metal "X" frame, inspired by classical furniture, and for its buttoned, black-leather upholstery. These pieces, perfectly proportioned, represent architecture in miniature and were exercises in new materials and space.

Between the wars, architects sharing a common outlook on both aesthetics and society began to design furniture for their buildings. Almost all architects of the Modern movement were socially conscious and considered progress the key to making the world a better place – more democratic and less elitist. However, the Modern movement was not represented by a particular group of people with a single manifesto (and hence is more precisely termed simply Modernism).

Although it was recognized in the 1920s and '30s (a period now termed Pioneer Modernism), the new spirit had been evolving prior to the start of the 20th century. As early as 1903, the Scottish designer Charles Rennie Mackintosh (*see* pp. 95 and 159–60) used the term when he explained, "The modern movement is not a silly hobby horse of a few who wish to achieve fame comfortably through eccentricity ... the modern movement is something living, something good, the only possible art." This is generally considered the first written reference to the term "modern movement," although it could be attributed to the architect and father of the avant-garde Otto Wagner, who, in Vienna as far back as 1894, when he became head of the *Akademie der Bildenden Kunst*, published a book, *Moderne Architectur*, in which he argued that modern life was the only point of departure for any creative artist.

The Vienna Secession

The new century encouraged in some a search for simplification and ease of living. A cleaner style, in reaction to Art Nouveau (*see* pp. 159–61), emerged in Austria and Germany. The Vienna Secession, founded in 1897, was a breakaway exhibition society primarily attracting avant-garde painters and architects, which sought to dissolve barriers between art and design, seceding from the conservative Academy in Vienna. The main aim was to procure private patronage in the absence of a supportive government programme and effective commercial gallery system. Its magazine *Ver Sacrum* called for unity of the arts, and a founding member of the Secession, Josef Hoffman (1870–1945) was one of the first to happily be referred to as "architect and decorator" (in *The Studio*). Other members, including Koloman Moser (1868–1918) and Josef Maria Olbrich (1867–1908), designed furniture, ceramics and metalwork. Mackintosh, who had begun to move away from designs of organic inspiration, exhibited a tea room with the Secession in Vienna in 1900. Having gained little recognition in Britain for his work, he was accepted by the members of the Secession, who elevated the importance of design through exposure at exhibitions. Instead of the whiplash curve that featured in Art Nouveau work, the straight vertical line became the dominant motif in Vienna. Simple room sets continued to form the core of Secession exhibitions until the group disbanded in 1905.

From 1903, Hoffman and Moser joined forces to found the modest Wiener Werkstätte, a crafts workshop. They were opposed to mass production and created precious objects for the wealthy. The Werkstätte's magnum opus was the Palais Stoclet in Brussels (1905–11) for millionaire banker Adolphe Stoclet, where a team of architect-designers, artists and craftsmen produced the ultimate "total work of art" on a budget that knew no bounds. Chairs and sofas were covered in chamois, walls were faced with yellow and brown marble, murals were painted by Gustav Klimt and mosaics were crafted in semiprecious stones. Despite the richness of the materials, there was, as in other Werkstätte commissions, a self-conscious emphasis on simple geometric forms. The unity between architecture and design was ever-present.

Although, stylistically, rigour and rigidity were making a statement in interiors, with rectilinear lines taking precedence over fluid Art Nouveau curves, for many there was something wrong: only the wealthy could partake in the new process.

The Moravian architect Adolf Loos (1870–1933, active in Austria) can be said to have been the first to reject ornamentation in interior design. Having spent three years (1893–6) in the United States, where he was impressed by the work of the Chicago School (particularly Louis Sullivan) and Frank Lloyd Wright at a time when Art Nouveau (*see* pp. 159–61) was ascendant in Europe, Loos set about debunking the florid overtones of what he considered excessive ornamentation. He also reacted against the luxury and cost of the Wiener Werkstätte interiors. However, he admired the British Arts and Crafts movement (which did not identify itself with Art Nouveau, only with the search for another style), as it did not embrace the excesses of its Continental counterpart. Loos's critical essay "Ornament and Crime" (first published in 1908 in *Neue Freie Press*, reprinted in 1920 in Le Corbusier's *L'Esprit Nouveau*) suggested the urge to decorate to such an extent was base and primitive. (He likened this kind of decoration to the criminal's tattoos and graffiti in

Below: The director's office at the Bauhaus, Dessau, Germany, is here pictured in 1926, the year following the school's move from Weimar. The chair is by Walter Gropius, who had made changes in the teaching staff by taking on painters Paul Klee and Wassily Kandinsky (whose influence can be seen here in the way that colour and pattern appear in the designs for the wall hanging and rug by the Bauhaus weaving workshop). The ceiling light is by Lásló Moholy-Nagy.

Above: The main salon of Pierre Chareau's 1931 *"Maison de Verre"* ("House of Glass") in Paris reveals his arrangement of furniture as if in a theatre, "where we are to be regarded as if on a stage." At the time, the press called it an "igloo." Exposed metal supports and a nonslip rubber floor are the setting for Art Deco furniture. The wall to the courtyard comprises an enormous screen of translucent glass bricks that give light but shield privacy.

public places.) Although the tone of the essay was not entirely serious, it did help challenge Art Nouveau designers who lived to decorate surfaces. Loos's writings and work in Vienna (where his domestic interiors included the Steiner House in 1910, the first house built in reinforced concrete) proved inspiration for the architects who went on to create the Modern movement.

Loos, who was not really part of the Modern movement although instrumental in reform, incorporated modest furniture into simple rooms, using built-in pieces wherever he could. He considered volume in his room plans, thinking about internal space and the play of vertical and horizontal planes. Key projects in which he experimented were the Moller House, Vienna, in 1928, and the Müller House, near Prague, in 1930, where he used split levels. The Müller House directly influenced later architects Richard Neutra, Rudolph Schindler and Erich Mendelsohn. Loos's 1907 American Bar (known as the Loos Bar) in Vienna was a very popular work, with yellow marble ceiling and green marble piers reflecting in cleverly positioned mirrors (customers were not reflected due to the height of the mirrors), giving the impression of greater depth in a limited space.

The Deutscher Werkbund

The German artist and architect Peter Behrens (1868–1940) was another with roots in the 19th century to inspire the Modern movement. His work linked art with industry. From 1908 (when he founded the Deutscher Werkbund, or German Work Association), with the support of Hermann Muthesius (1861–1927) and Henry van de Velde (1863–1957), Behrens gave the electric company AEG in Berlin a new identity: electric fans, clocks and kettles, graphics and factory architecture acquired a streamlined look. Le Corbusier worked in Behrens's office for a year in 1910, Walter Gropius in 1907–10 and Ludwig Mies van der Rohe in 1908–11 (all four Modern masters thus working alongside each other, briefly, in 1910).

The aim of the Deutscher Werkbund was to improve German design by bringing together manufacturers and artists. By 1910 there were hundreds of members, comprised equally of industrialists and artists. A great concern of the Werkbund was the improvement of mass housing. Conflict between members came in 1914, when there was a split between Muthesius and his supporters, who wanted design to be standardized, and van de Velde and his team, who feared that artistic inspiration would suffer. Van de Velde won the argument, indicating that the force of the Werkbund was in support of fine arts.

Van de Velde's side was led by Walter Gropius (1883–1969), who supported a Modernist aesthetic but also believed in artistic integrity. His extraordinary designs were noted by van de Velde, and as a result Gropius was made director of Weimar's art and craftsmanship school, the *Kunstgewerbeschule*. This was later to become the Bauhaus.

The Bauhaus

Perhaps the most potent symbol of Modernism – although history has been kind to the memory of the school, which could be faddish and experimental – the Bauhaus (literally "build house") developed a design style that incorporated new materials such as concrete and steel along with glass. It was established in 1919, when the fine and applied art schools of the *Kunstgewerbeschule* merged. At the helm, Gropius believed artists should train to work with industry, applying their "ability to breathe soul into the lifeless product of the machine."

The Bauhaus had a radical reputation, but was supported by the German government, which realized that reform in art education was necessary economically: the country relied on a skilled labour force to produce quality goods for export. In the Bauhaus manifesto, Gropius said: "The ultimate aim of the visual arts is the complete building.... These men of kindred spirit will know how to design buildings harmoniously in their entirety – structure, finishing, ornamentation, and furnishing."

When Gropius took on the Russian abstract painter Wassily Kandinsky (1866–1944) to run the murals workshop and the Hungarian Constructivist László Moholy-Nagy (1896–1946) to run the Basic Course in the early 1920s, the Bauhaus focus began to shift from crafts to Modern design; the result was seen publicly at a Bauhaus exhibition in 1923, which proved an enormous success. The new approach was exemplified by the "*Haus am Horn*," a house of steel and concrete designed by Adolf Meyer (1881–1929) and built in collaboration with George Muche, in which the emphasis was on function. The house formed a simple square with a central living space lit by windows in an upper storey. The Bauhaus made all fixtures, fittings and furniture; the kitchen was designed by student Marcel Breuer (1902–81), who incorporated continuous work surfaces, built-in cupboards and matching storage jars (already in production).

The school's reputation, in the vanguard of a new functional aesthetic, was confirmed in 1925, when it moved from Weimar to industrial Dessau and Gropius led the group in designing the new school building plus student and staff accommodation. This complex was the first large-scale public building of the Modern movement. The Bauhaus became the focal point of creative energy for more than a decade, and its long-term effects were far-reaching. Sparsely furnished schemes of little or no colour, where economy guides kitchen and bathroom fittings and all rooms are models of efficiency, as in the house Gropius designed for himself at Dessau, are valued in ultra-modern interiors today. Lamps from the Bauhaus, specifically by Marianne Brandt, functional and stylishly modern, and chairs (Marcel Breuer's "Wassily" chair, designed in 1925, is a favourite) have become Modern icons, coveted by collectors of 20th-century classics.

Below: Gio Ponti's glass fronted house at Via Dezza in Milan (1956–7) has screens as adjustable walls between rooms. At the table are "*Superleggera*" chairs from 1955 – so light that they can be picked up with one finger. On the left is a Hettner ceramic piece. The chest was painted by Edina Altara, and the painting is by Campigli.

Above: This cosy room set was devised by Alberto Pinto in France in the 1960s for a magazine photo shoot. Its design was based on the conversation pits that became popular in this era, when new and inexpensive materials were used and psychedelic colours started to come into play through youth culture.

In 1928, Walter Gropius resigned as director of the Bauhaus, to be replaced by architect Hannes Meyer. However, Meyer was considered too radical and too sympathetic to Communism, and in 1930 was replaced by Ludwig Mies van der Rohe (1886–1969), a popular choice following the success of his German Pavilion for the Barcelona Exhibition of 1929. None of the pavilion's surfaces were decorated but materials were luxurious – plate glass, marble and slate – and the structure allowed free movement. The chrome-and-leather "Barcelona" chair (since nicknamed the royal throne of America, having become *de rigueur* in offices and homes) and ottoman designed for the pavilion are significant for their refined details – the work of interior designer Lilly Reich, a teacher at the Bauhaus. She was to collaborate with Mies on many more projects, including the Tugendhat House (1930, Brno, Czechoslovakia), where the study and living area are divided by an onyx partition and a semicircular ebony screen surrounds the dining area. The "Brno" chair, designed for the project, was an exercise in creating graceful forms with steel tubing. Plain but sumptuous materials were used in the rooms, such as gray raw silk for curtaining and white kid leather for upholstery.

Mies had also worked with Le Corbusier. In 1927 both men, as well as Gropius, had taken part in a project in Stuttgart, Germany, with the Deutscher Werkbund. In all, 15 leading Modern architects participated, building 21 model dwellings.

Le Corbusier (1887–1968), born Charles-Edouart Jeanneret in Switzerland, changed his name and moved to Paris in 1920. Although untrained in architecture (he trained as a metal engraver but had the fortune to work in two significant architectural practices, with Auguste Perret in Paris in 1907–8 and with Peter Behrens in Berlin), for ten years he dedicated his efforts to perfecting architectural theory. He published two books, *Towards a New Architecture* (1923), in which he stated that a house was "a machine for living in;" and *Five Points of a New Architecture* (1926), which advocated the use of a "free plan" unrestricted by internal walls, large continuous windows, roof terraces, plain façades and columns or *pilotis* for support. Le Corbusier's Stuttgart buildings for the Deutscher Werkbund adhered to all five of these "points of architecture;" the apartments consisted of a single space that could be divided up with sliding partitions. The "engineer's aesthetic" was also evident in his "*Esprit Nouveau*" Pavilion at the 1925 Paris Exhibition and at the Villa Savoye on the outskirts of Paris in Poissy-sur-Seine, as was his commitment to readily available furniture (including bentwood chairs produced by Thonet). Le Corbusier created many of his influential furniture designs with Charlotte Perriand (born in 1903) and with his cousin, architect Pierre Jeanneret.

In the 1930s, the United States became the focus for Modern architecture and design. When the Bauhaus was closed by the Nazis in 1932, many staff, including Gropius, Breuer, Mies van der Rohe and Moholy-Nagy, emigrated to the United States (Gropius, Breuer and Erich Mendlesohn fled first to avant-garde Hampstead, in London, before crossing the Atlantic). The New Bauhaus formed in 1937 in Chicago. The Modern movement's international reputation was by then well established: in 1932 the Museum of Modern Art in New York had staged an exhibition that brought together Le Corbusier and Bauhaus masters from European countries, as well as from Russia and the United States. Their work had become known as "International Style" from the accompanying catalogue by Henry-Russell Hitchcock and Philip Johnson, who characterized it as avoiding applied decoration and having internal space that could be altered.

Union des Artistes Modernes

The *Union des Artistes Modernes* was founded in Paris in 1929 by Pierre Chareau, Robert Mallet-Stevens, Eileen Gray, René Herbst and others, who did not share the social aims of the Bauhaus and Le Corbusier or care much for theorizing, but welcomed the industrial materials and general ideas of the Modern movement. Mallet-Stevens instigated secession from the fading salon of the *Société des Artistes Décorateurs* to form what some considered the Parisian equivalent of the Deutscher Werkbund.

The French architect and designer Pierre Chareau (1883–1950) is best known for his "*Maison de Verre*," a house designed with Dutch architect Bernard Bijvoët and built in 1928–32. Using standard industrial components such as exposed iron beams and glass bricks – the latter, effectively concave lenses, transformed the internal lighting – it is made up of three levels connected by sliding and revolving doors. Chareau's furniture was often mechanical, incorporating wrought iron. His interiors included the salon of Mallet-Stevens's house in Neuilly on the Paris borders.

Gradually the austerity and staunch theorizing of the Modern movement was diluted. A spirit of confidence followed World War II, as the United States and Europe experienced an upsurge in living standards and the consumer age was born. The style dominating interiors in the 1950s and early '60s was "Contemporary," a symbol of newfound prosperity and progress. Contemporary style employed the vocabulary of its parent, Modernism, but swayed from its intellectualism toward an upbeat and colourful version in which open plan, picture windows, work surfaces, stylish lighting and kitchen equipment were concerns of the home owner and not just of the architect or designer, although design professionals had remarkable opportunities for creative expression, and this continued into the 1960s and '70s.

Contemporary had a strong visual impact and, unlike Modernism, was widely popular. Modernism had drawn public attention to the worst excesses of 19th-century design, and paved a way for acceptance of the new Contemporary approach to interior design and architecture.

Below: In this sophisticated high-rise apartment in Brazil, designed in the 1970s, Alberto Pinto worked in the vernacular of the time while creating a home of permanence and substance. Deep-weave rugs, built-in seating, globe-shaped furniture and accessories, and dramatic use of neon and reflective materials were all introduced into interior design in the late 1960s and '70s, when futuristic forms were inspired by space travel.

Eileen Gray

Eileen Gray's strength and character permitted her to work as an individual at a time when few women achieved anything comparable in the field of interior design. Unlike other female designers of the era – such as Lilly Reich, who worked with Mies van der Rohe, and Charlotte Perriand, who remained in Le Corbusier's shadow until recently – Gray pursued her own interests, although the desire for independence on both professional and personal levels was seen as eccentric. She was aided by financial independence, thanks to a privileged background. Born in 1878 in Ireland (to a titled Scots-Irish family), she spent her childhood in Ireland and London before emigrating to Paris in 1907. She lived in France until her death in 1976.

Starting her career with lacquerwork, Gray studied under the Japanese master Seizo Sugawara and in 1910 began work on decorative panels and screens, then furniture, desks, bookcases and beds. Regretting the exclusivity of her work, from 1914 she focused on furniture that could be batch-produced. She later worked as a designer and interior decorator, designing the Paris apartment of the fashionable dressmaker Suzanne Talbot, where luxury furniture was displayed with avant-garde work, and pieces for Elsa Schiaparelli and the Maharaja of Indore. From 1922 to 1930, she had a shop in Paris under the name "Jean Desert." In the late 1920s, having designed furniture for the oceanliner *Transatlantique*, she turned, at nearly 50, to architecture, at the suggestion of Jean Badovici, editor of the avant-garde journal *L'Architecture Vivante*.

Gray's seminal work, known as the "*Maison en Bord de Mer*," or E1027, was at Roquebrune-Cap-Martin in the south of France. There, assisted by Jean Badovici, she created in 1927–9 a "total work of art" incorporating her furniture and rug designs. The interiors were sparse, clean and comfortable; every space was multifunctional, with collapsible furniture in tubular steel, glass, plate glass and painted wood. The curious name E1027 was a code: the initial E for Eileen, followed by 10 and 2 to represent the tenth and second letters of the alphabet, J and B, for Jean Badovici; then 7 for G, the first letter of her surname. Le Corbusier and his wife Yvonne were frequent guests at Roquebrune. The house was handed over to Badovici in 1932, when Gray completed a house for herself, Tempe à Paille, near Castellar, also in the south of France.

Gray made highly personal use of the vocabulary of the Modern movement, and her later work is characterized by great flexibility of function and comfort. Her furniture was not mass-produced until the 1970s, but her "Bibendum," "Serpent" and "Transat" (for *Transatlantique*) chairs are now ranked among the greatest designs of the century.

BIOGRAPHY

1878	Born in Ireland.
1901	Began studying art at Slade School, London.
1905	Went to Paris to study lacquer artistry.
1910–14	Began to create furniture.
1919	Commissioned by Suzanne Talbot to decorate an apartment.
1922	Opened Paris gallery, Jean Desert, in rue Faubourg St Honoré.
1925–6	Designed "Transat" chair.
1925–6	Designed "Bibendum" armchair (ten originals known).
1925–9	Worked on E1027. Collaborated on "Garden of Rubies" for Mahar̄aja of Indore.
1930	Turned to architecture.
1976	Died.

Below: In the 21ft-by-46ft (6.4m-by-13.9m) living room of E1027, the divan converts to a bed, while a partition conceals a dressing room and shower. All furniture and rug designs are by Gray. On the wall is a marine chart.

Gio Ponti

The design impresario, architect and author Gio Ponti turned the Italian concept of "the good life" or *la dolce vita*, an expression implying post-World War II social and economic comfort and stability, toward the home and lifestyle. His work was modern in essence (he was a designer who embraced American Modernism), but it also drew heavily on traditional motifs and imagery, mixing the modern with the rich inheritance of the Italian decorative arts. His interest in the latter was expressed in his furniture decorated by Piero Fornasetti, one of his protégés. Ponti became Italy's best-known postwar architect; the Pirelli Tower in Milan (1956–8, by Ponti, Nervi and Associates) is an outstanding architectural work, its tapering contours and faceted shape echoing the architecture of Brazilian cities in a style far removed from the rectilinear post-and-beam construction methods that were popular in the United States at this time, which Ponti considered to be somewhat "unimaginative."

For over half a century Ponti's career included designing ship interiors, skyscrapers, sewing machines, tableware, fabrics, enamels, mosaics, plumbing fixtures and furniture, as well as elegant residences where modern material, process and construction would coincide with poetry and expression. His "*Superleggera*" chair for Cassina – meaning "super light" – is a 20th-century classic based on traditional furniture from the fishing villages of the Chiavari region of Italy. His Mediterranean sensibility brought vibrant colour to Modernism. "Here in the happiness of the tropics, modern architecture will flower, under perfect conditions for it," he said of Villa Planchart, a house he designed in Caracas, Venezuela, in 1955. His interiors were often decorated with trompe l'oeil paintings and incorporated tiles arranged in geometric patterns.

Ponti documented and determined the course of Italian design in his role as editor of the architecture and design journal *Domus*, which he founded in 1928 and edited until 1940, when he left to set up the art and culture magazine *Stile*. In 1947, Ponti returned to *Domus* (which had been edited in the interim by architect Ernesto N. Rogers), and proceeded to turn the magazine's focus back to the importance of the individual, at a time of surging mass production promoted by Modernism.

In 1928 Ponti published an article in *Domus* in which he extolled the Italian concept of living space. As he put it, "In the Italian home, there is not a great architectural distinction between the outside and the inside. In other places there is even a separation of forms and materials; with us the architecture outside penetrates the inside and does not reject the use of stone, plaster or frescoes."

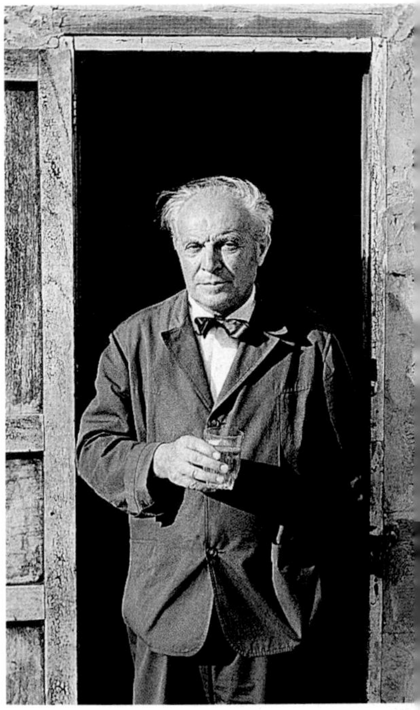

BIOGRAPHY

1891	Born.
1918–21	Studied architecture.
1921	Took job designing ceramics.
1928	Founded *Domus* magazine.
1933	Exhibited at Triennale.
1936	Built Montecatini building, Milan.
1936–61	Professor at Milan Polytechnic.
1940	Set up *Stile* magazine.
1947	Returned to *Domus*.
1951	Designed interior of liner *Andrea Doria*.
1953	Designed "Distex" armchair.
1956	Architect of Pirelli Tower. Designed "*Superleggera*" chair.
1972	Architect of Denver Museum of Modern Art, USA.
1979	Died.

Left: The dining room of the Parco dei Principi Hotel in Rome (now no longer in existence) was designed in 1964 by Ponti, with engineer Emanuele Porzio. As in an earlier hotel in Sorrento, ceramic pebbles are used as internal and external covering. The chairs are by Ponti.

Andrée Putman

"We manipulate space and functions, then everything is shifted around for several months and, a year after we have finished, a home becomes truly beautiful – an autonomous, living entity."

The French entrepreneur and designer Andrée Putman is probably best known internationally for her black-and-white palette of interior design, illustrated by the 1985 interior of Morgans Hotel in New York, commissioned by the entrepreneurs Ian Schrager and Steve Rubell. Morgans was the first of the new wave in the 1980s of fashionable hotels for the young and affluent; its scheme set the pace for hotel design over the next decade. Putman also designed the 1985 interior of the stunning and utterly modern Palladium nightclub in New York (architect Arata Isozaki). Its banks of television screens and twinkling fairy lights created a memorable stir in interior-design history.

Locally, in Paris and in France as a whole, the designer's image is quite different. Her 1983 scheme for the Paris office of the French Minister of Culture, Jack Lang, was widely publicized. Her museum interiors from 1987, the Musée des Beaux-Arts in Rouen and the Centre d'Art Plastique Contemporain in Bordeaux, are subjects of national pride. Passionate about preservation, Putman undertook the restoration of Le Corbusier's Villa Turque in La Chaux-de-Fonds in Switzerland. The Wasserturm Hotel in Cologne,

Left: Andrée Putman's ingenious design for an apartment for Jean-Paul Goude in Paris in the early 1990s included this wenge-wood bedroom, where four square pillars appear to support the ceiling but actually function as hidden storage areas so that the walls can be freed from the banality of more traditional closets.

Germany, which she completed in 1990, was a war-damaged water tower built in about 1870 by British engineer Charles Moore. In 1993 Putman redesigned the airplane Concorde's sleek interior with "the aim of removing all signs of frivolity, of self-importance, and replacing them with a more appropriate symbol of authority, that of elegance."

Putman's commercial interior-design assignments have included boutiques at the cutting edge of 1980s and '90s spartan chic: schemes for Thierry Mugler (in 1980–3), Yves St Laurent (in 1985), Balenciaga and Azzedine Alaia (in 1985). "I was the first to hang clothes on rails in my home and the idea translated. My own clothes were simple, in a monochrome palette, and I liked to see them, not hide them, for ease of dressing. It was a good discipline." Karl Lagerfeld, a close friend, has commissioned many projects, shops and homes (apartments in Paris and Rome). "It is only possible to design an apartment for a close friend," Putman often says, explaining that the design and decor of an apartment must reflect an awareness and understanding of its inhabitant. "It does not mean doing their portrait, but assisting them to create their own self-portrait, a task requiring a lucid and perceptive approach."

Andrée Putman was born Andrée Aynard, in Paris, between the world wars, and spent her early life absorbed in music and "over-exposed to art." Before she was four years old, she was attending a concert every morning, and at ten she was playing complicated pieces on the piano. "It was because I was not a virtuoso that I became interested in harmony and composition, for which I won first prize at the Paris Conservatoire, the highest award." Although she wanted to become a composer, a turning point came at the age of 20, when a professor suggested, "Hide yourself away for ten years and perhaps then you will manage to create a work." Putman gave up music there and then, "because that ridiculous caricature of the artist's work as a prison, the monastic idea of compulsory confinement, seemed unbearable." She has other early memories of home life with exotic parents, particularly of summers spent at Fontenay Abbey, near Dijon, which she describes as "visual arousal bordering on a spiritual experience." Putman attributes the strictness and linear nature of her architecture, which is an abstract and mathematical composition, to the disciplines of music, and makes reference to the vastness and beauty of Fontenay in explaining her understanding of space.

Early in her design career she wrote about interiors for the magazines *L'Oeil du Decorateur* and *Femina*, and in the 1960s was hired as a stylist by Denise Fayolle for the French chain-store Prisunic, where she pioneered well-designed

Above left: Putman believes that the bathroom is the core of a home; this example (in a hotel) indicates her love for the mathematics of design. The sink, a curved niche, hints at a fountain. **Right:** In the main room of Putman's own Paris apartment (1994), a chaise longue by Le Corbusier and a pair of 1930s ivory-decorated black lacquer tables by Drian show her admiration for 20th-century objects. The painting is by Bram van Velde.

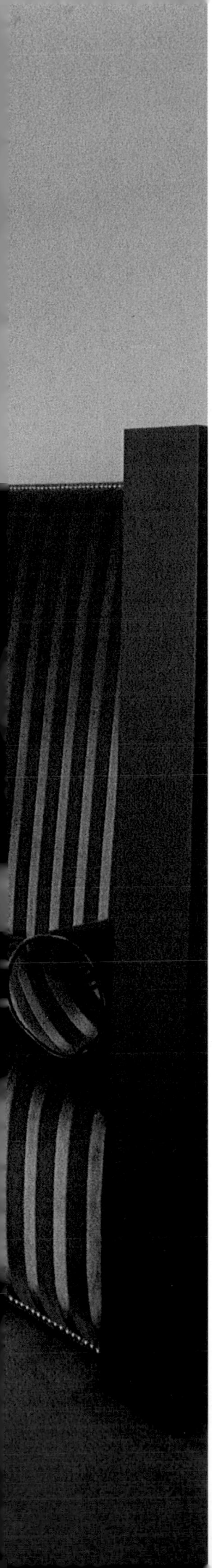

but inexpensive furniture and housewares. For Prisunic, Putman commissioned pieces from the talented artists Matta (Roberto Sebastian Matta Echaurren), Pierre Alechinsky, Bram van Velde, César and Jean Messagier, who between them designed a range of products, including lithographs, fabric patterns and tableware.

An early house commission came in 1963, when Andrée Putman was selected to decorate the home of Michel Guy, later French Minister of Culture. In 1968 she joined the partnership of Maime Arnodin and Denise Fayolle, called MAFIA, where she designed interiors, textiles and furniture. In 1971, in collaboration with Didier Grumbach, she designed both home furnishings and clothing for the shop Createurs et Industriels, which specialized in showcasing work of young fashion designers.

In 1978 Putman, together with Jean-François Bodin, established the design firm Ecart (a backward spelling of "trace" – intended as a word play on the company's objective of tracing the best of earlier designs), along with the furniture firm Ecart International. Ecart International developed to reproduce the furnishings of the 20th century's most prominent designers, among them Pierre Chareau (*see* p. 99), Michel Dufet, Mariano Fortuny, Eileen Gray (her carpets and chairs; *see* p. 100), René Herbst and Robert Mallet-Stevens. Ecart International produced a combination of these classics and the contemporary designs of Sylvain Dubuisson, Patrick Naggar and Sacha Ketoff. Putman's own furniture was issued by De Sede, her lighting by Baldinger and fabrics by Stendig. Putman is a self-proclaimed "amateur archaeologist of modern times," without whose ability for talent-spotting,

Left: A war-damaged water tower in Cologne, Germany, became the elegant Wasserturm Hotel (1990) at the hands of Putman, who redesigned the interior. In its suites, semicircular chairs echo the cylindrical form of the building. **Above right:** The windows are porthole-like. A console following a window's curve serves as a desk or dressing table when the folding mirror is pulled up. A screen lifts at night to cover the porthole.

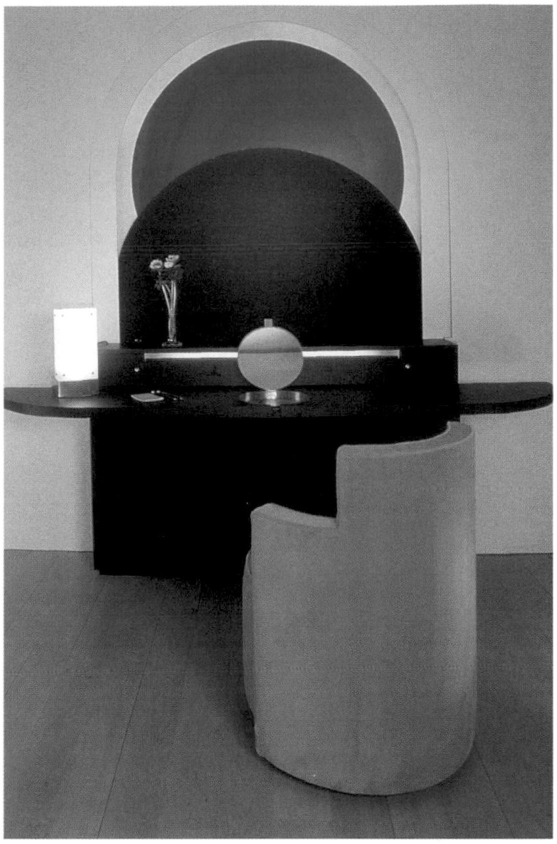

1980s and '90s interiors would look very different, and a great many cafés and restaurants worldwide would not boast the chairs they do today.

By 1998 Putman was no longer with Ecart but was as prolifically creative as ever, proclaiming: "The revolution in my work now is the care for human touches." Based in a transformed courtyard house in Paris, she and her team work on a range of projects: an information centre in Chile; a hotel in Germany for Volkswagen; and a collection of furniture and objects for the Furniture Co, an arts-based design community showcasing in New York. Putman was awarded France's prestigious *Grand Prix National de la Création Industrielle* in 1995, and received Honorary Doctor of Fine Arts degrees from Parsons School of Design in 1996 and the School of the Art Institute of Chicago in 1998. Film has also become a part of the designer's life since 1993, when she created an imaginary world in the form of an interior set for Peter Greenaway's film *The Pillow Book*. Her work continues to be noted for its vibrance and variety.

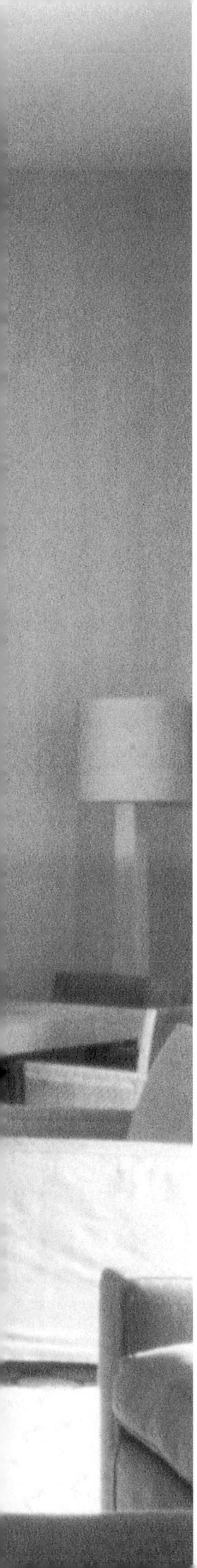

Peter Marino

"My passion is painting and these are my paintings, my tableaux. I have a heavy art-history background which, coupled with the architecture, explains what I do.... My methods are more like those of a painter, especially the layering, than of a traditional architect."

It is testament not only to Peter Marino's talents but also to his interpretative abilities that many demanding clients, influential taste-makers themselves, have turned to him to design domestic and professional spaces. The New York architect has created images for homes, stores and offices for a list that reads like a Who's Who of the fashion world: Valentino, Christian Dior, Giorgio Armani, Louis Vuitton, Calvin Klein, Yves Saint Laurent, Chanel, Fendi, Gianni Agnelli and Donna Karan. Marino sees no conflict of interests: "A good law firm would take on all these clients, so why not an architect?"

Publicly he is best known for Barneys stores in Los Angeles, Chicago, New York and Tokyo. His sleek 1998 Donna Karan store brought a slice of Manhattan speed to London's Bond Street. In New York, he renovated the Public Library, and St Patrick's Cathedral on Fifth Avenue. Accolades have included American Institute of Architects awards for Armani and Americana stores, a Landmark award for Barneys, and Fashion Group International's 14th Annual Night of Stars "Master of Design" award.

Having begun studying fine arts, Marino moved to architecture because of "a prejudice that architecture is by far the greatest art," and obtained a

Left: In Giorgio Armani's Milanese palazzo, architect Peter Marino lined the salon in oak, and mixed custom-made furniture from Bologna with vintage Jean-Michel Frank pieces sourced in Paris. The cubic benches, by Frank, are covered in silk-velvet fabric woven by James Gould in Connecticut.

Bachelor of Architecture from Cornell University in 1971. He worked for Skidmore Owings & Merrill, George Nelson and I. M. Pei/Cossutta & Ponte, before founding Peter Marino + Assoc in 1978. The firm has grown to employ 95 staff, in offices in New York, Philadelphia, East Hampton and, in Britain, London. Its first project was artist Andy Warhol's New York house, for which payment was in pictures: "He knew art was business."

Marino's passion for art crosses the centuries. "I love Spanish and Venetian painting, it makes me insane. I love outlandish French Rococo painting – really good Boucher and Fragonard. I like any statement of truth and clarity." His favourite contemporary architects are Norman Foster, I. M. Pei and Nick Grimshaw. "Rem Koolhaas's work is new: it implies movement and avoids static spaces.

Above: The checkered effect on the wall of Armani's library was hand-painted by artist Kimiko Fujimura. A pair of walnut and goatskin cabinets stand one on each side of the Minnesota limestone fireplace. The straw chairs, plaster and parchment lamps, and white-leaded oak desk are by Jean-Michel Frank. **Right:** Armani decided to preserve the existing grid wall in his neat, luxurious master bathroom. The goatskin stool is by Frank.

But the New Moderns are getting further from people, more abstract. I don't want to look retro but I am not in the Koolhaas school of deconstructivism – it is interesting architecture as sculpture but people don't always have a place in it."

He has expanded Modernist vocabulary to embrace cultivated sensitivity to particulars of client concerns, period, history and site: "In the early 20th century, decoration was stripped away and there was a rationalism to Modernism; it made sense and was a new style. But after World War II, people began to work in the 'style' of Modernism, not the content. There was a backlash and people asked, why not review all historic styles? That brought about the confusion we are in now. New Modernism can be very violent – architects use violent words: 'implosion,' 'explosion.' Why does everything new have to be hyperactive?"

Current projects include new concepts for Chanel, Guerlain ("Really exciting. We'll be using holograms.") and jewellers Fred, all in Paris. As an image creator, Marino feels the world is full of talent and competition, but he can (and will) do anything.

Even if incorporating old items, Peter Marino interiors are intended to look "like something never created before." His work often has a marked masculinity, yet is warm and comfortable to live in, and rarely too austere. The sample board (*right*) shows elements typical of his designs, exemplified in the principal bedroom of an apartment designed for Giancarlo Giammetti, chief executive of fashion empire Valentino, in central Rome. Taking up the top floor of a palazzo, this apartment is designed around an extensive art collection that includes works by Modigliani, Picasso, Matisse, Francis Bacon and Andy Warhol.

Wall decor

Textured horsehair panels custom-woven in France **(1)** with mahogany supports **(2)** provide the frame to the room. A collection of black-and-white flower photographs by Robert Mapplethorpe adds drama, as does the focal point of the room: a painting by Tony Sherman **(3)**.

Woodwork

The *Empire* bed is flanked by cabinets **(4)** by Josef Hoffmann. Sand-blasted oak doors (not shown here) lead to the walk-in closet and bathroom.

Bed covering

The striped throw on the bed **(5)** is a cashmere shawl from Guatemala.

Floor covering

The matting **(6)** is custom-woven linen, its pattern modelled on African cloth. (African textiles complement early-to-mid-century designs and colours, particularly Art Deco.)

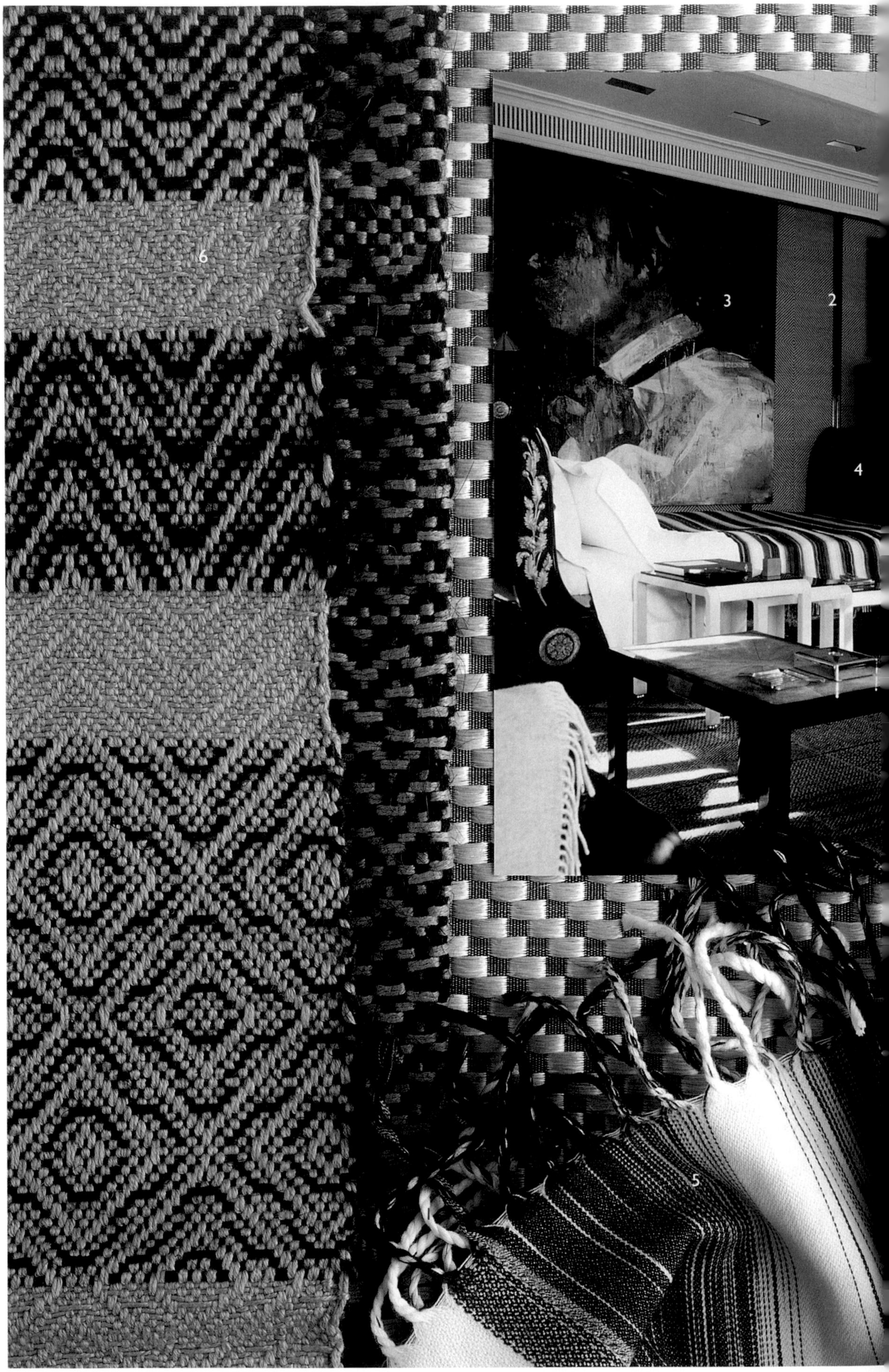

Design signatures

Marino believes that house decoration should not be like set design; temporary decoration lacks integrity. He creates homes of permanence, with "correct" architecture as well as decoration, and a seamless fusion of structure and interior.

Quality

The one characteristic that binds Marino's many and varied projects is more easily recognized than defined: quality. All materials used are of the finest calibre. He likes antique textiles, complexity, volume and overlaying, and often designs when he is at the opera. Whether working in modern vernacular or with traditional furniture, he combines materials in a highly original fashion.

Colour

Growing up in New York, Marino was inspired by weekly visits to the Metropolitan Museum of Art. He is still influenced by museum pieces and by the colours and concepts of works of art. His palette varies according to the project, although he favours neutrals (bone, beige, sand) combined with rich, dark woods. When using true colour, his preferred shades have great depth.

Texture

Often using clients' art collections as a starting point, Marino builds up textures and colours gradually: antique textiles with the latest fabric collections, or rough-hewn carpets in neutral tones juxtaposed with luxurious chenille and cashmere. Texture matters to him, and he likes to mingle many weights of fabrics in one room (provided the room's basic design is strong enough).

Versatility

Marino is versatile, and able to interpret people's wishes. There is no "Marino look;" each client's style is freshly created for them alone.

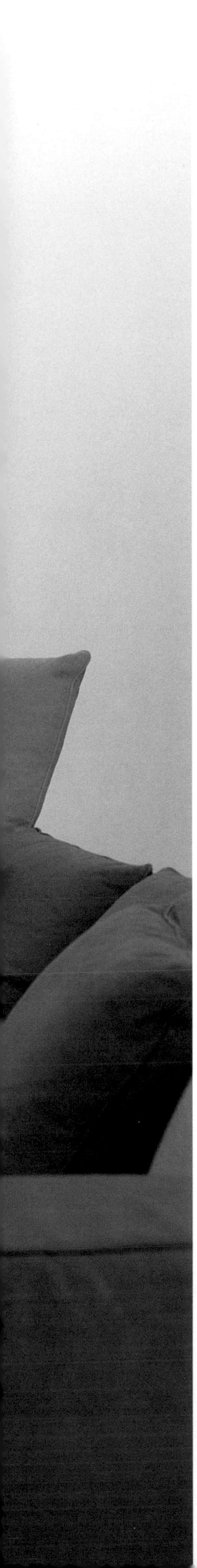

Christian Liaigre

"The most important element of my work is the sense of calm in a turbulent world. Too many objects distract. We're all bothered by too much stress in our lives – interior design should break with all that."

French interior and furniture designer Christian Liaigre, known in the design world as the "Zen Master," believes the purpose of design is neither to pamper nor to provoke, but "to soothe." Born in 1943, Liaigre spent his first years in the quiet of the Vendée in western France – "a Protestant region where people didn't have the means to live any other way than simply" – where his father bred horses. Yet local ship owners brought exotic finds from their travels, and Liaigre's visual experience was a combination of the rustic and the refined. "Everything else was Louis XVI or Louis XV – together it was an extremely seductive mixture."

Liaigre studied painting at the *Ecole des Beaux-Arts* in Paris and graduated from the *Ecole des Arts Décoratifs* in 1968, but baulked at working in art or design: "Being a decorator back then generally meant little more than painting houses." He left to raise show horses in Bordeaux, only returning to Paris in the late 1970s when offered an art-direction position at the home-furnishing firm Nobilis. But he was soon frustrated at the firm's reluctance to produce his designs, and in 1987 he unveiled his first boutique on Paris's Left Bank, showcasing his own pared-down furniture,

Left: The first house Liaigre built totally was for a Japanese/Thai couple in Bangkok in the early 1990s. He combined rigorous architecture, his own mellow style and Thai tradition. The salon has a light oak floor. The "*Baptiste*" sofa is covered in ecru linen; wenge side tables and pewter "*Lanterne*" lamps are by Liaigre. The painting is by Miguel Barcelo.

inspired by fascination for African and Polynesian cultures – furniture which precipitated the tribal look that has featured in home collections of designers such as Donna Karan, Ralph Lauren and Pierre Frey. Liaigre's "Nagato" stool, a minimalist piece carved from a single block of oak, became a signature of his furniture design. In the late 1980s he single-handedly launched a vogue for wenge, a dark African wood, to which Italian furniture-design giants gave their blessings at the Milan Furniture Fair ten years later. (Architects, including minimalist John Pawson, then began to use wenge.)

High-profile commissions followed the boutique's success, including fashion designer Kenzo's Paris loft (heavily Japanese-influenced). As a commercial designer, Liaigre furnished Lloyds in London; French embassies in New Delhi, Warsaw and Ottowa; the Societé Generale de Belgique in Brussels; Julien Cornic art bookshops in Paris and Tokyo; a modern art gallery in Bangkok; and the Hôtel Montalembert (once home to politician and writer Count Montalembert, now said to be the most elegantly modern hotel in Paris). In 1998 he completed the restaurant Shozan on avenue Montaigne in Paris (where, stylistically, modern meets colonial Asian) and The Mercer hotel in New York's SoHo district, where urban strictness is softened by textured furnishings and peaceful hues. Of the latter, Liaigre comments, "It's simple, quiet, chic – what one wants to find in one's own home."

As well as spearheading minimalist interiors, Liaigre shows skill in blending early modern with new. The Villa Martel, a house originally designed by Robert Mallet-Stevens (*see* p. 99), on Paris's rue Mallet-Stevens (a street constructed in 1926), underwent a sensitive three-year restoration and rethink at the hands of Liaigre and its owner, art expert Karsten Greve. Greve commissioned Liaigre because he knew he would "respect the identity of the space and not betray the original style," following the dictum of Mallet-Stevens that "decoration must be intimately linked to action.... By its ambience, it defines the individuals who live there." But the colour palette is typically Liaigre's, with grays, browns, taupes and off-whites: the overall effect is serene and harmonious, the result a modern masterpiece that transcends time.

Above and above right: The lobby and suites of The Mercer hotel in New York's SoHo have signature Liaigre lampshades. **Right:** The "collection room" in the Bangkok house opens onto the dining room, where doors and Thai-style slats to let in a breeze are in ebony. Wenge *"Long Courrier"* dining table and *"Grec"* chairs, and black saddle-leather and linen curtains are all by Liaigre. The suspended bronze-and-silk lamps were designed by Liaigre and made specially for the scheme.

Shelton and Mindel

"We started working in the city. When you work in a city, space is at a premium, so we had a big education and we took our big education and applied it to very small places. It is better that way."

The New York architectural firm Shelton, Mindel & Associates is known for its comprehensive architecture, interiors and product design for corporate, cultural, academic, retail, recreational and residential clients. The name is associated with clean, timeless interiors that juxtapose and refine modern and classical elements. Lee Mindel, who names Finnish architect Alvar Aalto (1898–1976) and Pierre Chareau (*see* p. 99) as early inspirations and Richard Meier, Frank Gehry, John Pawson and the Gwathmey Siegel team among current ones, was heralded by other design professionals in the late 1990s for the treatment of his own living space – the penthouse of a former hat factory in the Flatiron district of Manhattan, which showcases the most salubrious and alluring elements of Modern design.

Both partners of the firm completed formal training in architecture. Peter Shelton studied at the University of Pennsylvania and Pratt Institute (graduating in 1975), then worked for the New York architecture firms Edward Durrell Stone & Associates and Emery Roth & Sons. Lee Mindel obtained a degree in architecture at the University of Pennsylvania, followed by a Master's from

Left: The living area of Mindel's apartment in New York's Flatiron district has a fireplace framed in steel and structural glass, and floors that are oak inset with cherry. His choice of objects reflects his enthusiasm for early-to-mid-century Modernism; the round table and bookcase are by Jean Prouvé. Lamps are designed by Shelton, Mindel & Associates for Nessen.

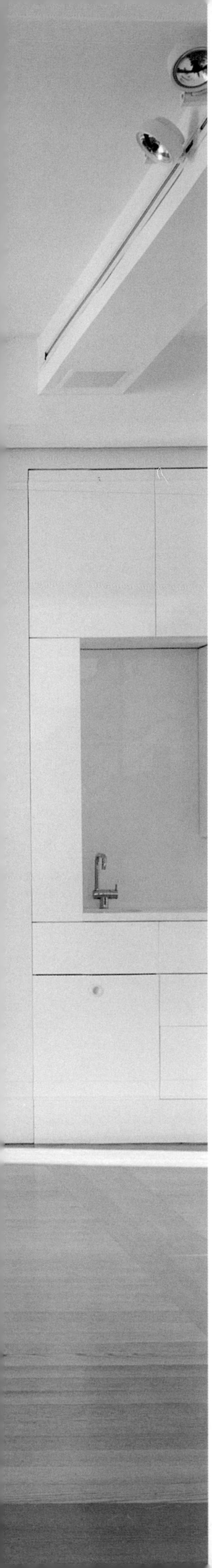

Harvard in 1976. He worked for the New York architecture firms Skidmore, Owings & Merrill and Rogers, Butler, Burgen before partnering Shelton.

The Shelton and Mindel design philosophy is clear, and is applied to all projects, whatever the scale. "In the beginning we thought metaphorically about spaces and how to solve problem spaces for very humble jobs, and tried to bring that level of thinking we had been trained in across the board to all levels of jobs, whether the job was a bathroom or an apartment renovation. Later it would be a new house or a cruise ship," says Mindel. Since its inception in 1978, the firm has received five AIA (American Institute of Architects) distinguished architecture awards, five Interiors awards for residential and corporate interiors, three Roscoe awards for product design (which included table and upholstery collections), an *Interior Design* magazine "Hall of Fame" award, three Society of Registered Architects awards and a Progressive Architecture citation. The firm's design process is tripartite, from "project genesis," dedicated to gathering and absorbing information from all sources available; through "architectonics," where rules of design are constructed to protect the integrity of the concept; and finally to "execution," in which the goal is simple but the reality relies on dedication and thoroughness.

Such dedication, along with flexibility, one-on-one working relationships and originality, helped win the firm an enormous commission in 1992, when Shelton, Mindel & Associates was selected over more obvious contenders to design the 170,000sq ft (16,000sq m) international head-quarters for Polo, Ralph Lauren in New York.

Left: Next to the dining area in Mindel's apartment, Hans Wegner's "Ox" chairs form a seating area defined by a V'Soske rubberized canvas mat. Basswood doors slide to conceal a bar and storage. **Above right:** The living area has a Fritz Henningsen-designed wing chair and a sofa by Antonio Citterio, behind which stands a console by Jean Prouvé. The coffee table is by Paul Kjaerholm and the kite lamp by Pierre Guariche.

These qualities are also important in dealing with domestic clients – many and varied commissions for apartments and houses have included work for financier Robert Soros, Hollywood moguls and style guru Troy Halterman (of the SoHo, Manhattan, furniture and accessories store Troy). Halterman and his wife commissioned two homes, one a light, spare and polished but comfortable Long Island ranch house and the other a pristine and highly evolved Upper East Side New York apartment that fuses Shelton and Mindel's purism and clarity with the Haltermans' own taste.

In the impeccable, crisp penthouse apartment he has created (with associate architect Reed Morrison) for his own living, incorporating steel and structured glass, Lee Mindel has absorbed original classics by early-to-mid-century Modernists: a table by Jean Prouvé, dining chairs by Josef Hoffman and Hans Wegner's "Ox" chairs. A bench by Antoni Gaudi seduces visitors entering the apartment through the cylindrical gallery to the dining and living areas. A sweeping stainless-steel staircase leads to a rooftop pavilion. Curiously, a glass chandelier created by Syrie Maugham (*see* p. 63) in the 1930s for Venini, a commission for Lord Mountbatten's house in London, presides over a dining table designed by Shelton and Mindel.

Mindel explains his passion for incorporating beloved objects into the starker surrounds of his interior spaces. "We are going through a post-minimalism where there is a desire to live in a clean way but also to have access to things that make you feel good, where you are not a victim to those things – where there is storage and where you can have something to remind you that it isn't an absent world. Objects have to be treated like objects and not become set decoration, or they seem like an anachronism. If an object does not seem to be solving anything or doing anything, it gets in the way of life. Nothing must stifle the space; everything must enrich."

Shelton and Mindel let the space and architecture drive: "We don't start out with decoration. The decoration is just one brushstroke of the larger canvas. Historically, there were decades of acquisition in which each acquisition became glued into the interior environment and then the artistic sense of that object was completely lost because the space became that object, was overtaken by it. Decoration ultimately becomes part of the vocabulary of style, but emerges through the architecture as a solution to a problem, as opposed to a means to an end."

In looking at resolving problems, how architecture and interior relate, and how each element when looked at in a textbook manner does what it is meant to do, the Shelton and Mindel team question and answer very simply: "Similarly to the way literature or music is created, if there isn't a large idea or a running theme and a structure that is consistent and carries throughout, the piece falls apart. It just doesn't sustain itself. Architecture is a

discipline – an art that transforms space." This art is applied by Shelton and Mindel at every level from site planning, landscaping and architecture through interiors and objects.

Like the Modernists whose furniture Mindel collects, he is committed to the all-encompassing possibilities of design, "although it is hard within your own context to have a historical perspective. Did Le Corbusier step back and look, or just move on? Once you allow a little distance you can be conscious of design. You think of Le Corbusier's deep philosophy and how it carried through: his spaces really worked and are valid now."

For the maverick and engaging Lee Mindel, privilege means having rooms that work. Discipline is a luxury he values. Another is openness to change: "Just like fashion, things change. A space that can change and evolve, as we constantly need to be doing, is certainly the ultimate luxury."

Above: In a bedroom in Troy Halterman's New York apartment, the bed is covered in pale French-blue satin. The two-armed lamp is by French lighting designer Serge Mouille. **Right:** Halterman's sitting room overlooking Central Park features a white, surf-board-inspired "Orgon" chair by Australian Marc Newson, a low limestone table by Shelton, Mindel & Associates, a 1984 cylindrical lamp by Castiglioni and an ultrasuede sofa.

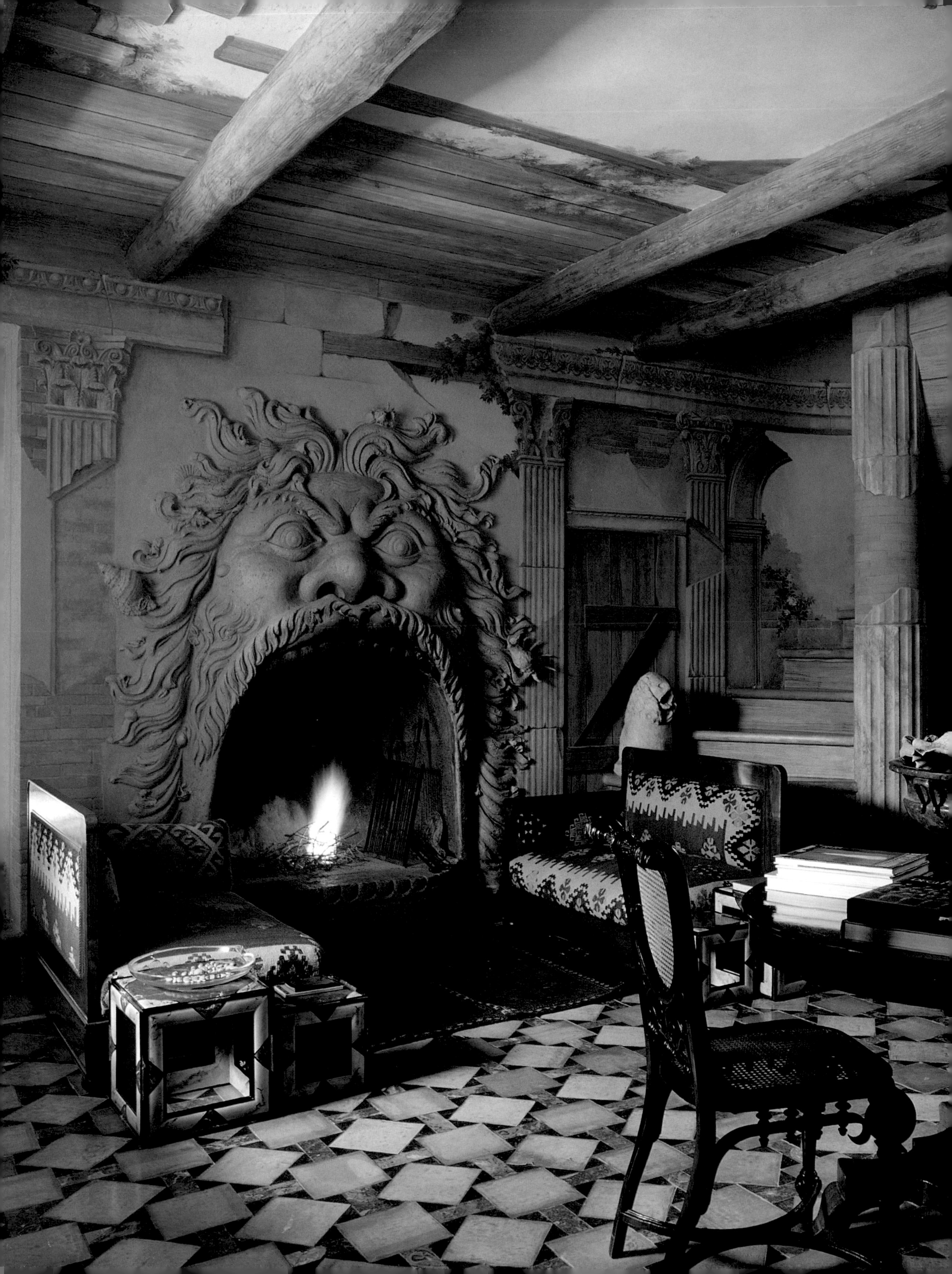

ECLECTIC

The eclectic interior is a milieu where a sense of theatre prevails, where fantasy knows no bounds but where balance is found among the overstated, the bizarre and even the irrational. In the early 20th century, larger-than-life experiments in decoration were born out of set and fashion design, which had been influenced by expressions of freedom in new dance forms, by avant-garde and Fauve painters, and, particularly, by the Surrealists. Today, eclecticism in interior design is highly colourful and spirited, and still features the artfully unexpected.

Above: To enter a salon by Paul Poiret, such as this, wrote Cecil Beaton in *The Glass of Fashion*, was to enter the world of *The Arabian Nights*: "In rooms strewn with floor cushions, the master dressed his slaves in furs and brocades and created Eastern ladies ... the counterpart of ... the pageantries of Diaghilev."

Previous pages: This tower room with gargantuan fireplace is by the master of the theatrical approach to design, Milanese architect Renzo Mongiardino (died 1998). Famous for floridly painted rooms that allowed the exterior to enter the house, he drew from ancient sources – Greek, Roman and Etruscan – as well as the work of Bernini, Palladio and Borromini.

A taste for the exotic and whimsical took hold at the start of the 20th century, in ballet, art, fashion and consequently interior design. Persian and Arabian themes became fashionable, and the Ballets Russes' staging of *Scheherazade* in Paris in 1908 spawned a passion for the mysterious, the glamourous and the erotic. Sumptuous, plump cushions in tactile fabrics were scattered in the most formal townhouses, colours became stronger (with black and red predominant), lacquerwork and Chinese lamps found popularity, and tassels finished everything from pillows to tablecloths. Fashion and art showed similar trends and, briefly in 1905-8, the Fauves (especially Henri Matisse and Raoul Dufy) used vibrant paints and expressive strokes.

A key player was Paul Poiret (1879–1944), an *haute-couturier* and entrepreneur famous for helping to liberate the female body from the corset (by loosening and lowering it) and designing costumes for actress Sarah Bernhardt. His fashions, influenced by the Orient and *Directoire* style, featured high waistlines, embroidered frock coats, turbans, aigrettes and harem pants. In 1912, Poiret formed the design workshop Atelier Martine. Its output was influenced by the Wiener Werkstätte (*see* p. 95), and for a while Dufy designed its fabrics. Poiret also amplified the colourful, naive work of the working-class girls attending his *Ecole Martine* art school in his atelier creations. The atelier produced fabric, wallpaper, ceramics, textiles, furniture and interior-design schemes for homes and boutiques. Poiret and his followers liked furniture to be low, almost at ground level, evoking decadence. Poiret used his couture showroom for dazzling parties attended by his *beau-monde* circle, including painter André Derain and liberated dancers Isadora Duncan and Regina Badet. He created theatre sets, and redecorated three barges for the 1925 Paris Exposition with fabric-tufted ceilings.

Armand-Albert Rateau (1882–1938), known for Art Deco interiors, also designed a beautiful but bizarre apartment for couturier Jeanne Lanvin in Paris (1920–2), with remarkable furniture in verdigris bronze strewn with butterflies and daisies. The apartment led to the design of the Lanvin fashion house, where Rateau came to manage the department of interior design. In 1926, he famously decorated a bathroom in Madrid in gold lacquer, bronze furniture and fur-covered chairs.

Surrealism

Surrealism had its inception before World War I, when painters like Salvador Dali and Matisse sought to realize the philosophy that life could be changed by depicting the workings of the subconscious, that only unreason can give us art (this was not new: Romantic writers such as Coleridge experimented with drugs to uninhibit the mind). The results could be monstrous and disturbing, and the Surrealist Exhibition organized by English collector Roland Penrose at London's New Burlington Galleries in 1936 found the public unprepared. However, further exhibitions – "Fantastic Art, Dada and Surrealism" in New York, and a Surrealist event in Paris in 1938 in the form of *tableaux vivants* and theatrical sets – contributed to flights of fancy across the arts. The best-known survivor in furniture is the "Mae West lips" sofa (1936, by Dali, made for Edward James [*see* below] by Green & Abbott, London; James also commissioned the "Lobster" telephone from Dali). Five other versions of the sofa were ordered, for Elsa Schiaparelli's salon and for Jean-Michel Frank (*see* p. 65), who put them in a private cinema-cum-ballroom with walls painted pink, blue, sea-green and yellow to casually blend with the scarlet carpet.

Carlos de Beistegui (1896–1970, scion of a wealthy Hispano-Mexican family and patron of decorative arts in France) caused outrage with his Paris apartment overlooking the Place d'Etoile (1931–6, featured in 1936 in *Architectural Review*). Part way through the project, he replaced architect Le Corbusier (*see* p. 98) with Emilio Terry (1890–1969); the final effect was out-of-scale and surreal. A spiral staircase led to a roof terrace with blue walls, artificial grass that served as a carpet for mock-Baroque furniture, and an outdoor fireplace with a mirror above. Inside, the only light was from candles; chairs were glass, and upholstery on white-and-gold Second Empire settees was ice-blue.

Englishman Edward James (1907–84), an art collector and patron, developed Surrealist interiors in his three homes: a townhouse in London's Wimpole Street, a Gothic castle in Berkshire (which he surrounded by marble grand pianos hoisted into trees), and Monkton (a 1902 house by Edwin Lutyens) in Sussex. Monkton was transformed to James's fancy in 1934–8: the exterior was painted violet; chunky-wave-patterned fabric enveloped the entrance hall and bedroom gallery; other walls were fabric-padded and buttoned, like a luxurious padded cell. The master-bedroom walls were hung with fine silver netting and the radiator was hidden by chainmail.

Meanwhile in New York, in 1932, Bruce Butterfield created a Surreal backdrop for Juliana Force and her eclectic Victorian and Regency collections. The Whitney Museum's first director, Force lived in a Victorian building above the galleries at 8 West Eighth Street: gargantuan lamps and tasselled ropes on pulleys hung from her sitting-room ceiling and furniture was far from sober.

While not inspired by Surrealism, newspaper magnate William Randolph Hearst's New York home, the Clarendon Apartments on Riverside Drive, was rich in drama. Hearst acquired the 10th, 11th and 12th floors of the building to house a growing family and burgeoning art collection. As family and collection grew, he took over more floors, and in 1913 bought the entire building. By the early 1920s he had created a French Empire bedroom and a triple-height sitting room modelled on a vaulted Gothic chapel; the house had become monumental in proportion and peculiarity.

Below: In a bedroom by Paul Poiret, from 1924, fantasy is given an airing. A simple, low bed on a platform is draped in exotic tasselled fabrics evocative of the Orient, and flora and fauna enter the scene by way of a painted tree and scattered blossom on the walls and a somewhat surreal snailshell on the ceiling.

Rose Cumming

Rose Cumming (1887–1968), a self-taught decorator, like many of her contemporaries, found the fashion for the "Old French Look" overplayed and stale. Natural flamboyance made her excel in the creation of fantasy interiors inspired by Surrealism and Hollywood movies. Where some women decorators were called "untrained," Cumming was more "untamed."

Arriving in New York from Australia toward the end of World War I – en route to England, where she was to be married – Cumming had a long wait for a passage. She met the Editor of *Vanity Fair*, Frank Crowninshield, who suggested she become a decorator. She allegedly replied, "First tell me what it is?" Crowninshield introduced her to decorator Mary Buehl.

In 1929 Cumming wrote, "Interior decorating is the frivolous sister of the architectural profession. It requires primarily that one be an expert in colour, design, period, and in the placing of furniture.... A decorator should, in addition, be blessed with a sixth sense – a kind of artistic alchemy which endows the articles of furniture with that elusive quality of livableness which transforms houses into homes."

Her taste was eclectic: she enjoyed Gothic and 16th- and 17th-century English furniture, early Oriental furniture and art (except Indian), Chippendale, Louis XV, Austrian Baroque and early painted Venetian, and was "especially fond of early Victorian, Regency and *Directoire* furniture, old mirrors, glittering chandeliers and highly polished floors." A bird of paradise herself, with violet-dyed hair, she would add Oriental birdcages, ornamental frogs, mice, monkeys, horses, fruit and vegetables, miniature furniture and wax figurines. Her potpourri rooms bordered on extreme, but were always gleamingly "Hollywood."

Where possible, Cumming used candles in preference to electricity – which, along with modern architecture, she claimed not to understand. She also disliked wall-to-wall carpeting and low ceilings.

She came to love America when, four months after opening her shop on Madison Avenue, burglars stole every piece of furniture. The papers reported the loss as $5,000, and a note arrived that day from "a friend" with a $5,000 cheque. Cumming only learned her benefactor's identity 25 years later.

The shop's distinctive window displays were noted by press and public, and Cumming's house on 53rd Street, with theatrical mirrors and black candles, became a talking point. Her design trademarks were silver-foiled paper applied to walls, smoked mirrors, and vividly coloured patterned curtains. She decorated homes across the United States, and in Britain, Australia and New Zealand. Since her death, Rose Cumming Ltd has continued in business, and sells fabric and furnishings.

BIOGRAPHY

1887 Born in Australia.
1917 Left Australia for England but found herself stranded in New York. Met Frank Crowninshield.
1920s Worked for Mary Buehl, then at decorating studio Au Quatrième at Wanamaker's store, New York, before opening her own shop on Madison Avenue.
1968 Died.

Below: The bedroom of Cumming's New York apartment (1946) mixes period furniture and fantasy, with signature shimmering walls. In her lifetime, the position of furniture in her home was unchanged for over 25 years.

William Pahlmann

"With the exception of psychoanalysis, there is probably no other field of civilized endeavour in which the personalities of client and advisor are in such violent conflict or harmonious cooperation as interior decoration," claimed Bill Pahlmann. For over a half a century, Pahlmann, master of "modern Baroque" (his term), exercised a pervasive influence on American taste. Known for the "Pahlmann eclectic look," he was the first to design model rooms for department stores. Some rivals considered his work pretentious and even insane, but they conceded that it was elegant. When he received the Elsie de Wolfe Award from the New York chapter of the American Institute of Interior Designers in 1964, the introduction read: "Except for Elsie de Wolfe, no one has influenced home decoration more than Mr Pahlmann."

William Pahlmann was born in 1900 in Illinois. When his father died, the family moved to San Antonio, Texas, where at ten he started drawing and arranging flowers for the Baptist church. In his first job (travelling salesman for a sewer-pipe company), he took a correspondence course from *Arts and Decoration* magazine; in 1927, he moved to New York to study at Parsons School of Design.

He set up on his own in 1931 in New York – an early customer being the first Mrs William S. Paley – and went on to head the decorating department at the store Lord & Taylor. He lived well, and was an ardent party host. In the 1950s he bought a modern house in Westchester County, in upstate New York, which became a showcase for design.

Believing that "the customer is usually wrong," Pahlmann trusted his own taste, and had a roaming impulse to experiment. He introduced blond Swedish wood, furniture on wheels and coasters, shaggy carpets and overscaled lamps. For outdoor parties, he draped walls in satin and grouped low tables, skirted to the floor, on bright Victorian carpets. In the army in World War II, Pahlmann transformed the officers' club in cerulean blue, chartreuse and brilliant red, using twill from army fatigues, specially re-dyed, with spatterdashed high-glazed cabinets, shell motifs and screens. Not all his work was glitzy: some rooms had brick walls and tweed fabrics, or hollow, square tubing as candelabra.

In 1946, he set up William Pahlmann Associates in New York, decorating and designing furniture, wallpaper and drapery. He also wrote a newspaper column, "A Matter of Taste," and was Interior Design and Decoration Editor on *Harper's Bazaar* magazine – where his first article began, "The well-dressed house is too rare in this country of well-dressed women." His firm contributed to exquisite Manhattan restaurant interiors: the Four Seasons (architect Philip Johnson) and the Forum of the Twelve Caesars. Dorothy Tremble, Anne Winkler and George Thiele all worked in his office.

BIOGRAPHY

1900	Born in Illinois.
1906	Moved to Texas.
1920s	Job as a salesman.
1927–8	Studied at Parsons School, New York.
1929	Studied at Parsons School, Paris.
1931	Opened New York shop.
1936	Head of decorating department, Lord & Taylor, New York.
1946	Set up William Pahlmann Associates. Began writing articles.
1955	Published *Pahlmann Book of Interior Design*.
1959	Collaborated on Four Seasons restaurant, New York.
1987	Died in Mexico.

Dorothy Draper

BIOGRAPHY

1889 Born in New York.
1920s Designed houses in Tuxedo Park, New York.
1925 Set up Architectural Clearing House.
1929 Worked on Carlyle Hotel, New York.
1930s Designed hotel interiors, including The Greenbrier, West Virginia.
1940–5 Columnist for *Good Housekeeping* magazine; also radio producer and author.
1954 Designed restaurant for Metropolitan Museum of Art, New York.
1960 Sold business.
1969 Died.

American decorator Dorothy Draper is most often associated with The Greenbrier hotel in White Sulphur Springs, West Virginia. The country's top hotel for over a century, it has welcomed international dignitaries as well as the fashion set (Pierre Balmain used it to launch clothing collections). Its interior in the early 1930s was the epitome of American grandeur, blooming in a palette of grass green, turquoise blue, sugar pinks and scarlet, with stark white backgrounds; Draper favoured abundant stripes, checks, lattices and designs of flowers the size of cabbages. Not for the faint-hearted, this florid interior – updated by Carleton Varney of Dorothy Draper & Company, Inc, a world-renowned decorator in his own right – still attracts attention.

A woman of boundless confidence with a work ethic to match, Draper was born Dorothy Tuckerman in New York, in 1889. In the 1920s, having renovated her first home, in Manhattan, she began designing houses. In 1925 she set up the Architectural Clearing House, matching architects to commissions, and in 1929 designed public areas of the Carlyle Hotel in New York. The idiom she adopted there has been called "Roman Deco."

Her boldness attracted attention, and she came to specialize in hotels. Projects included the Mark Hopkins Hotel, San Francisco (1935), the Camellia House in the Drake Hotel, Chicago (1940), the Quitandinha resort, Petropolis, near Rio de Janeiro (1944), and rooms for the Statler chain. For New York's Metropolitan Museum of Art she designed a Roman-inspired restaurant. Ever energetic, she had a radio programme and wrote books and articles.

The Draper look inspired the majority of American textiles and furnishings in the 1940s–50s. Her most popular designs were "Scatter Floral" and "Brazilance" (both 1947) and "Stylized Scroll" (1940s). Surrealism was evident in her use of scale and deliberate confusion of the internal and external – at the Hampshire House Hotel, New York (1936), interior function rooms were designed as exterior space, featuring the façade of a Georgian house and garden furniture. Draper's business acumen balanced her theatricality, and her style was wholly American.

Right: Larger-than-life colour schemes (here a room in The Greenbrier hotel) and use of chunky floral patterns designed by Dorothy Draper instigated an entirely new look for domestic and commercial interiors in America in the 1940s and '50s. This style echoed a new-found postwar optimism that dared to appear in Europe only in highly diluted forms.

Billy Baldwin

Widely considered the father of modern decorating in America, Billy Baldwin's colour sense was inspired by the paintings of Henri Matisse, who he believed "emancipated us from Victorian colour prejudices." Baldwin was responsible for the decor of songwriter Cole Porter's apartment – with tubular brass bookcases and French family furniture in a predominantly classic English scheme, on the 33rd floor of New York's Waldorf Astoria hotel – as well as for homes in the 1960s for Paul Mellon, Greta Garbo and American *Vogue*'s most illustrious editor, Diana Vreeland. Capote said of the Cole Porter apartment that Baldwin had "transformed it into an island of sublime and subtle luxury."

Born in 1903, William Baldwin studied at Princeton University, and then became an interior decorator; he was already established in Baltimore in 1935, when Ruby Ross Wood (*see* p. 30) asked him to join her New York decorating practice. He made the move to New York in style: his home was one of the townhouses on Sutton Place whose façades had been painted black by Dorothy Draper (*see* p. 130). A highlight of this period came in 1938, when Baldwin collaborated on the Surrealist interior of a house in Montego Bay, Jamaica.

After Ross Wood's death in 1950, Baldwin went into partnership with designer Edward Martin, forming Baldwin and Martin in 1952 (later Baldwin, Martin and Smith). There he mainly designed residential interiors, although his debt to Wood was clear in his use of crisp settings with plain white walls as a backdrop to antiques and contemporary components, and bare floorboards supporting simple matting and elaborate carpets. He also adhered to Wood's belief that a home should show the life and taste of the character who lived there. Later, in the 1960s, he still favoured plain walls but treated them with colour; glossy brown vinyl was a particular passion and trademark. He introduced this into Mr and Mrs Lee Eastman's apartment, calling it "noncompetitive but deeply comfortable; a beautiful unifying backdrop for paintings and people" – they had huge Rothkos, de Koonings and Klines. Albert Hadley (*see* pp. 72–7) held that Baldwin was America's most sought-after decorator in the 1960s.

Respecting his industry, Baldwin saw it as one of service: "I like eccentricities if they are the eccentricities of the owner. If a client wants a 19th-century Gothic library, it is up to me to create the best 19th-century Gothic library ever done, whether I like it or not. Or it's up to me to furnish an ultramodern house to the best of my ability."

Baldwin believed perfection to be sterile, flouted "unhappy mediums," and knew "good taste has no price tag." He taught at Parsons School of Design from 1950, and was a consultant at New York's Cooper-Hewitt Museum and a member of the President's Council of the Museum of the City of New York. He wrote several books: *Billy Baldwin Decorates* (1972), *Billy Baldwin Remembers* (1974) and *Billy Baldwin, An Autobiography* (1985). One of his happiest moments was hearing Van Day Truex (*see* p. 73) say of his work, simply, "It is a statement."

BIOGRAPHY

1903	Born in Baltimore, USA.
1920s	Graduated from Princeton University.
1935	Joined Ruby Ross Wood's New York firm.
1938	Designed Surrealist interior, Jamaica.
1945	Returned from army; started to write for US *House & Garden*.
1952	Partnership with Edward Martin.
1957	Designed residence in Cuba for sugar magnate Senor Puerco.
1963	Jacqueline Kennedy became a client.
1970s	Began writing books on interior design and decorating.
1984	Died.

Above: Billy Baldwin's own home was true to his tastes, and clearly reflected his policy of avoiding "the deep-freeze atmosphere of the museum."

Madeleine Castaing

"My style is the style which was current just before my birth. I started to love houses ... at the age of eight. Nostalgia isn't so bad, it allows you to express things which come from the heart."

Decorator and antiquarian Madeleine Castaing (1895–1992) left a lasting impression on all who knew her, through her personality as well as her work. With her startling black bob and exotic, impeccable make-up (ostrich-like eyelashes and crimson lipstick), she presided over her dark, quasi-Victorian Paris gallery, on the corner of rue Bonaparte and rue Jacob on the Left Bank, until well into her nineties, and was often to be seen at her desk in the lamplit window or poised on a small chair. Daring to be different, she was immortalized not only in her own designs but also in the work of her friend, photographer François-Marie Banier, for whom she was a constant inspiration.

The shop, unchanged to this day, is now under the watchful eye of her grandson, Antoine Castaing, and Madame Laure Lombardini, loyal to the firm for 40 years. "She was inimitable," says Antoine of his grandmother. "She would place together pieces of furniture and *objets* from many places, and had an astute sense of scale, especially small scale. She had, simply, the knack. It was not always easy to recognize pieces that appealed to her – exquisite chairs from Russia, lamps in turquoise and green, tiny black tables, patterned carpets – but together

Left: The blue salon or games room in the first-floor apartment at rue Bonaparte has a white sponge effect on the walls: having primed them for fabric, Castaing liked the effect better than the fabric. The blue-and-black carpet, the curtain fabric and the brocade on the chairs are all by Castaing, while the raised height of the curtain pull-back is typical of her work.

they formed a harmonious picture." Lombardini adds that she had "such a sense of humour. But one thing Madame Castaing did not like was cut flowers of any kind – she felt flowers belonged outside."

Castaing's style reflected her background. For 54 years she was happily married to Marcellin Castaing, a businessman with a passion for literature and art. Madeleine had grown up near Chartres, spending holidays at St Pré with her grandfather, whose house she loved. It was as a child that she first saw the house at nearby Lèves which she and her husband later bought. The Castaings were very active in Parisian society, but Lèves became their main home, although it was taken over by Germans in the war and had to be bought back afterward. Madeleine gave the grounds a sculpted quality – arches, statues and clear vistas – along with a sense of wilderness. Designs were softened by ivy tumbling over balustrades, in an echo of interiors Castaing was to create. She became so fond of ivy that even in plastic form it would occasionally feature in her rooms.

In 1936, the couple bought an old laundry in Paris on rue du Cherche Midi. It remained empty until 1941, when Madeleine opened an antiquarian shop. In the occupied city, she saw a need for a feeling of "home;" as luxuries dwindled and people sought escapism, Parisians flocked to her window.

After the war, Castaing visited Britain with her son Michel and discovered English furniture. An admirer of pan-European taste of the late 18th and early 19th centuries, she placed Biedermeier with Napoleon III and Regency with Russian, adding a few glass lamps and curious artifacts.

The shop moved to rue Bonaparte in 1947 and was painted black. (The small *entresol* group of rooms above it became the couple's Paris base, redecorated in 1948 and still intact today.) Black and blue-green became Castaing's signature colours. She was both decorator and antiquarian, and more: Jean Cocteau and Castaing together decorated his house at Milly, near Paris, and in 1966 she built a pagoda to be exhibited at the Grand Palais in Paris.

In the late 1960s, Marcellin Castaing died. Madeleine moved into the main first-floor apartment above the shop, decorating it with a panache that assured her reputation. The flat now belongs to film-maker Ismail Merchant, who used it in 1996 as a set for *La Propriètaire,* starring Jeanne Moreau.

Artists, musicians and poets were drawn to Castaing, among them the painter Chaim Soutine, who lived at Lèves for 18 years. Castaing was the greatest collector of his work, and one of his portraits of her is in New York's Metropolitan Museum of Art. Her talent lives on in those she worked with; decorator Jean-Louis Riccardi, her former assistant, pays homage to her in his colourful work.

Above left: Detail from the pink-and-gold bedroom in the first-floor apartment; Chaim Soutine's painting *"La Sieste"* hangs over the bed. **Right:** The same bedroom. The furniture is predominantly Napoleon III, 19th-century gilt. Panels on the bedroom doors show the fabric *"Nuage,"* a design that came into being as a result of an accidental water leak onto a bolt of fabric. François-Marie Banier has left a message on the mirror.

Bellissima
François-Marie

FLOWER ARRANGING
JAMES GIBBS

David Hicks

"Couturiers have been highly influential in my life. They have the best taste. Chanel and Givenchy – look at Givenchy's Paris apartment. What Balenciaga did was pure architecture, and Bill Blass's drawing room is one of the most spectacular ever seen."

Interior designer David Hicks was one of Britain's great exports to the United States, in design terms, although he lived mostly in England (his apartment or "set" at the Albany in London's Piccadilly appeared in magazines with varying decoration over the years) and had properties in Portugal and the West Indies. His influence was global. With his architectural approach, he spawned a generation of interior designers who covered chairs with horsehair and leather and spurned flowers.

Left: David Hicks's well-proportioned family home in Oxfordshire shows the essence of Hicks style: geometrically patterned carpet and other identifying features, including tell-tale pink walls. Older family possessions – such as ancestral portraits – and elegant chairs are incorporated into the otherwise new design.

Billy Baldwin (*see* p. 131) commented that Hicks's bold carpet designs "revolutionized the floors of the world." His "tablescapes" (arrangements of *objets* on tabletops) characterized his work, as did his dramatic lighting. Mark Hampton (*see* p. 31) worked with Hicks at 21 before going to McMillen Inc; Stephen Ryan and Charles Bateson learned their skills from Hicks before starting design firms in Britain.

Born David Nightingale Hicks at Coggeshall, Essex (near London) in 1929, son of a stockbroker, he went to boarding school at Charterhouse in Surrey, which he loathed, then studied at Central School of Art and Design in London. After serving in the Army Education Corps, where he taught art, Hicks became an independent interior designer

in 1953. There followed a brief spell at the advertising agency J. Walter Thompson, then his career was launched in 1954 with a feature in British *House & Garden* on his mother's London house. A lucky break came with an early client, Lady Benson, widow of magazine publisher Condé Nast. For four years from 1956 Hicks was in partnership with Tom Parr in Hicks and Parr (Parr later headed Colefax and Fowler), before setting up David Hicks Ltd in 1960, the year he married Lady Pamela Mountbatten, daughter of Lord Mountbatten. In 1970 he set up David Hicks International Marketing Ltd, with offices in Belgium, Switzerland, France, Germany, Pakistan and Australia. He first created his geometrically patterned carpets and textiles in the 1960s, and 1966 saw publication of *David Hicks on Decorating*, the first of nine books. In the 1970s and '80s he turned to household objects, clothing, costume jewellery, shoes and eyeglasses, through David Hicks Association of Japanese Manufacturers. His work on domestic projects spanned the continents; he was at ease designing in Athens, Barbados or New York.

His appearance was as inspiring as his designs: in the 1960s and '70s Hicks donned red-heeled shoes or patent boots, leather trenchcoats and bright silk and velvet clothes, although he was equally at home on a shooting party. His pronouncements on taste were irresistible; forever theatrical, he loved to entertain. His influences included: "the man with perhaps the greatest taste in the world, Wright Luddington, in Santa Barbara, who had enormous Greek statues. But the biggest influence was my mother-in-law, Edwina Mountbatten, who brought an American over to England to 'do her house.'" Nell Cosden designed the Mountbattens' home "in no particular period. She had an enlightened mind and mid-19th-century taste." Others were Madeleine Castaing (*see* pp. 132–5), John Fowler (*see* pp. 29–30 and 34–9), Renzo Mongiardino and Rory Cameron. Van Day Truex (*see* p. 73) was both inspiration and fan, delighted by Hicks's bold, precise use of colour.

Hicks's clients ranged from the Rolling Stones to Queen Elizabeth II (a bachelor suite at Buckingham Palace for young Prince Charles, and Gatcombe Park for Princess Anne). Vidal Sassoon, Douglas Fairbanks and Helena Rubinstein (an apartment in fuchsia, pink and orange) were also clients. Hicks left his stamp on ocean liners (the 1969 nightclub on the original *QEII*), jets and cars – BMW commissioned him to look over car interiors.

In the late 1990s, Hicks turned for a few years to garden design and writing books. He had just returned to interior design, and was finishing two houses in Bloomfield Hills, Michigan, when he died in 1998. He had planned his own funeral over a period of four years, its specifications laid out in a notebook entitled "David Hicks's Demise," and had even selected the fabric to line the coffin – a testament to his inimitable style and wit.

Above left: A bedroom in Hicks's Oxfordshire house has a half-tester baldaquin over the bed in the same jazzy fabric as the bed covering and curtaining. **Right:** At a villa in Portugal an up-to-the minute soft-sculpture artwork by Rib Bloomfield contrasts with classical elements. Hicks helped pioneer "tablescapes" and "chimneyscapes" (curios attractively grouped on tabletops, chimneypieces or consoles).

As shown in the sample board (*right*), David Hicks introduced indigenous materials into his interior scheme for the Villa Verde in Portugal, along with some favourite elements that work successfully in city and country alike.

Fabrics

The curtains in the drawing room, approached through the dining room, are of simple, light-weight but voluminous unlined silk taffeta in "tobacco" colour. The fabric firm Pongees (often used by Hicks) today produces a dyed Habotai silk in various shades of brown **(1)**. This kind of fluid curtaining diffuses light, is unstuffy, remains elegant and helps to keep a room cool in summer. A light wool in hot fuchsia **(2)** covers the sofa.

Walls

A tone away from the sofa colour, walls are painted in John Oliver's vivid "kinky pink." A neutral is selected for the adjoining room **(3)**.

Flooring

The smart Brussels weave carpet **(4)** designed by Hicks was made by Avena carpets and produced specifically for this project. Hicks produced many designs for fabrics and carpeting using repeating stamps of geometric forms. The cool *molyanosh* (a Portuguese term) floor in the dining room, again in geometric pattern, is composed of limestone, light oak and terracotta **(5)**.

Furniture

The tripod table in limestone with a *molyanosh* granite top was made locally in Portugal. In the background, the exaggerated obelisk cabinet is a typical Hicks signature piece.

Design signatures

The keynote of a David Hicks design is a sense of individualism, sometimes within a traditional framework, but more often in contemporary idiom. Even in the late 1960s, his style seemed radical compared with that of his contemporaries.

Fabric

Fabric was a salient feature for Hicks: he believed that "nondescript rooms and furniture can be changed in a flash by using the right stuff for the curtains and furniture." Plain fabric was not anathema to him, but he was masterful in his use of pattern, and favoured texture combinations: "linens, glazed chintzes, velvets, cottons, ottomans, slubby weaves and sailcloths." The only shiny fabrics allowed were glazed chintz and pure silk damask.

Pattern combinations

Hicks advised conviction when mixing patterns. "Good sources of inspiration are the pattern mixes of Van Gogh, Matisse and Vuillard. You only have to look at an old patchwork quilt or Oriental costumes to see the charm of pattern with pattern."

Colour

Blocks of plain colour identify a Hicks interior. He favoured beiges, grays, dark brown, gunmetal and coffee, with splashes of "brilliant Chinese yellow, shocking pink or flame orange." For the more adventurous, "colour on colour" was advised: reds and pinks together, oranges with browns, or yellows and blues with each other and with green.

Placement of objects

"The clutter of possessions, whether valuable or inexpensive, can be a hindrance or an advantage depending on how they are arranged." Hicks believed cold, bare rooms to be lifeless; with a disciplined eye, pictures could be hung and objects placed as "controlled clutter" on tabletops.

THE CITY SHAPED
Los Angeles
A HISTORY OF MODERN ART
GIO PONTI
ANDREA PALLADIO

John Stephanidis

"Sometimes, I imagine, training can be a hindrance, makes one too strict, unable to be flexible – I like to be able to change my mind.... Everywhere teaches you something."

Versatile designer John Stephanidis is untrained in the field and has not worked for anyone else; believing that "eye" is more important than anything, he has culled his visual talent and experience from years of world travel. "People neglect to look and educate themselves. If you have gone to Rome, then go back to Rome, continue to look, and look again; by the fourth time you will see it. You assimilate and then regurgitate – it is not immediate but that is what happens."

Left: In John Stephanidis's home in Cheyne Walk, Chelsea, London, an antechamber to the bedroom has a statue of Alexander the Great by Canova and architectural features inspired by Borromini. The "Rothschild" chair in fake leopard, "Eaton" geometric table, painted faux-marble bookcase and carpet are all by Stephanidis.

He relies upon his library, his constantly updated scrapbooks of cuttings and postcards of colourful images (including a Picasso postcard: "Picasso was the greatest decorator ever – his colour and texture.") and storyboards. He has a 20-strong team, including architects, to back him up, and especially values his head designer, Gaël Camu.

Stephanidis is behind many more seminal designs than most people know. His inventions include the "swimming pool on the edge," where a pool is filled to the brim and is at one with its surroundings. He respects innovation – "Norman Foster's extension to the Royal Academy (London) is brilliant: the insertion into the old building" – and places where the new is accepted. "England is

cramped. So much is old, so much is conversion in town and there is no point in building in the country because there are lovely places to buy. I don't really approve of the trend where buildings are turned into something else: I appreciate preservation of old buildings, but in spirit I prefer the new." Places like Australia have an attraction, "a spontaneity that comes from self-assurance and a better climate."

His beginnings were exotic. "When children in London were going to the British Museum, I would be visiting the Pyramids." His Mediterranean childhood inspired an acute sense of sight and smell, and an understanding of the changing nature of light; to "consider how to illuminate a room with both daylight and electric light" is often a starting point for him. Like Elsie de Wolfe (*see* p. 62), who started the rage, Stephanidis prefers light switches near the floor, "about 90cm above," so as not to interfere with placement of pictures or furniture.

John Stephanidis was born to Greek parents in Cairo in 1937. The family, originally from the island of Corfu, had lived in Egypt for three generations. His father was in the British Military Mission and some of Stephanidis's early childhood was spent in Eritrea. His parents' house in the port of Massawa on the Red Sea had a garden cooled by a vast trellised cube, a design of latticework which appears frequently in his later work.

He went to school in Cairo (the English School at Heliopolis, which had students of all races and creeds; Stephanidis studied Arab history as well as the Christian Bible). Images from those early days had a lasting impression, from the textures of stucco walls to Alexandria's Mediterranean-weathered corniche. The clear, watery light of Alexandria and the dusty, desert light of Cairo are still clear in his mind years later.

At university in Britain, studying Politics, Philosophy and Economics at Oxford, Stephanidis longed for the spirit of Egypt and abroad. He still seeks out the exotic – evident in his furniture design, some of which is wittily and purposely derivative. His furniture, carpet and fabric designs have been frequently copied, and his teak and light-oak chairs have spawned a plethora of similar pieces made more cheaply and without such attention to detail ("I find it all rather flattering."). The simple moulded wooden "Malcontenta" chair (named after the Villa Malcontenta) and furniture of colonial inspiration are among the most popular.

Above: The master-suite sitting room in Cheyne Walk contains a 1920s Russian chair, a Tang Chinese horse and a Russian mirror. **Above right:** The library in Cheyne Walk boasts a painting by British artist Ray Richardson and a French 18th-century table with a myrtle bush. **Right:** The guest suite of a townhouse, Upper East Side New York, has a 1940s *médaillon* cabinet by Jean-Michel Frank, a table by Eileen Gray and an armchair by Stephanidis.

Some designs are distinctly his: a Turkish coffee tray has become an inimitable Stephanidis trademark. For ten years in the 1980s he had a shop in Fulham Road, London, where he sold his own fabric, carpet and furniture (also distributed in the United States).

Now based in London's Chelsea, Stephanidis concentrates mainly on private homes (from low-budget houses in Greece to chalets in Switzerland), also designing show apartments and commercial projects including rooms at Claridges Hotel, London. He has also written books: *Rooms: Design and Decoration* in 1986 and *Living by Design: Ideas for Interiors and Gardens* in 1997. His staff plan architecture and interiors meticulously: "I don't know how many in this profession do as we do. If you have no training, you haven't an idea of how others function." Tomes of plans, renderings, sample boards and facts and figures are collated before a stick of furniture is brought into the picture.

Stephanidis lives in Britain (in London and Dorset, in the southwest). His country home, Cock Crow, was near-derelict when he happened upon it 20 years ago, ivy-clad cowsheds facing each other across a broken concrete yard. Now it is a home of rusticity and charm, with Mediterranean lightness and ease. East and west wings were added to connect the cowsheds, the west wing forming a shaded loggia with a mysterious door. Contrasts create sophistication: the combination of openness with shutters, the rooms shaded yet light. Lawns, box hedges and chestnut trees encircle the buildings, along with a water garden, terraces, a wisteria-clad pergola and a bamboo grove. Garden-designer friends such as Arabella Lennox-Boyd helped – "You must listen to people about a garden."

Left: Although the main theme in the vast New York townhouse is strongly Beaux-Arts neoclassical, the guest suite is based on the 1920s, and the quality of materials used evokes the era. Silver-plated door furniture and hinges embellish the rosewood door, while the carpet – woven especially for the scheme – was created by John Stephanidis in collaboration with his head of design, Gaël Camu.

The vision is one of composure; influenced by America, where "comfort has always been more important than in England," Stephanidis aims for luxury in simple surroundings by paying attention to *petits soins*, small points. His rooms are chameleons: simple blue-and-white summer chair slipcovers are removed in winter to reveal rich fabrics, tartans, red felts and maroon wool with dark rich velvets. Ikats cover upholstery. In one of his homes, printed batik fabrics from Indonesia hang behind a bed in a room with Le Corbusier chairs and a Marcel Breuer table; the effect is harmonious: "It is not just a case of going to India and picking something up. It is so much more than that."

He always has new projects, and is proud of ex-employees who have started their own firms – Philip Hooper, Carolyn Trevor and Anthony Collett. He is in awe of architects such as Frank Gehry (he sees Gehry's Bilbao museum as "a vision," a classic of the 20th century) and anyone whose work is truly new: "Philippe Starck – Delano's hotel in Miami – he designed the whole thing, every detail, and it is magnificent, very glamorous and original."

Stephanidis's achievements are global, but some of the greatest are near to home. For three years he designed the Duchess of Westminster's vast home, Eaton Hall, in Cheshire. In her twenties at the time, the Duchess was "not so conventional" about decoration, yet the designer had to work with family treasures as inspiration. Stately rooms in rich fabrics – leopard and moiré – combine with cooler rooms where colourful mosaic floor and pillar designs are emblematic of the characters of the occupants and their bold designer. "People interpret their styles differently, they should live in a reflection of their creativity;" Nancy Lancaster (*see* p. 32) at Haseley Court, Francis Bacon in his painting studio, "both are valid." Other clients are high-profile, including the Gettys, Lord Glenconner (Colin Tennant) and Lord Rothschild, yet Stephanidis always feels there is more to do.

Jacques Grange

"I tend to live in what I am doing rather than in the image I am reflecting. I still question myself. I create places of mood, I'm interested in form and materials – the woods, the 'substance.'"

A man of multifaceted talents, French interior architect, decorator and furniture designer Jacques Grange has termed his own style "classic reinterpreted," while others have called it "beyond fashion." Grange has worked miracles with some of the most prestigious homes in the world, creating forums where the boldest furniture in existence blends with gentle pieces of differing origins and ages. He has put together homes for clients such as Isabelle Adjani, Yves Saint Laurent (for whom he has completed eight projects, including homes in Morocco and in Deauville, France, as well as *haute-couture* boutiques in Paris and the avenue Marceau fashion house), Pierre Passebon, Paloma Picasso (shops in New York and Paris, and her Paris home), and Princess Caroline of Monaco (her private yacht, *Pacha III*, in 1990 and her Monaco residence in 1996).

Born in 1944 in Saint-Amand Montrand, south of Paris, the son of an engineer, Jacques Grange was schooled at the *Lycée Janson-de-Sailly* and the *Ecole Gerson* in Paris before attending both the Boulle (for four years) and Camondo (for a year) schools in Paris. There he learned his craft and came to love 19th- and 20th-century art and

Left: In the dining room of the Paris apartment, containing essentially 20th-century pieces, where Grange lives, he displays curios and furniture to evoke a 19th-century spirit. Elements include an 18th-century Russian theatre chandelier and early 19th-century Russian chairs upholstered differently in jewel colours. The library links the dining room to the salon.

objects, which he now collects (ceramics are particular favourites). In 1965 he worked with the great French decorator Henri Samuel, before taking a position in 1967 with Alain Demachy and Didier Aaron. He is still affiliated to Didier Aaron, but has practised independently since 1970. Early commissions in the 1970s came from Princess Ashraff Pahlavi for homes in Paris and in Juan-les-Pins in the south of France. Paris's Casino de Divonne followed, then a home for Sylvie Vartan and Johnny Halliday (France's top singing star) in 1974. Grange also worked on three floors of the Lloyds insurance building in London, and in Paris on the Museum of Decorative Arts at the Louvre, an office in the Palais de Justice (1985) and the chic restaurant L'Avenue on avenue Montaigne (completed in 1991). His accomplishments have earned him the title *Chevalier des Arts et Lettres* from the French Ministry of Culture.

Above: The salon of the Paris apartment is comfortably elegant, with an armchair by Paul Iribe, one of a pair. A Christian Bérard painting is reflected in the mirror above the fireplace. **Right:** The bedroom has a stripped *lit à la polonaise* (named after the Polish wife of Louis XV), with a 1937 banquette by Ernest Boiceau, and a leather-and-metal *chauffeuse* chair by Eric Schmitt.

Grange perceives his own work to be in the vein of Henri Samuel and Renzo Mongiardino, "both true masters of decoration.... It would probably be all the better if I had an influence. But I don't, although people do inspire me: Christian Bérard for his magic, Jean-Michel Frank (*see* p. 65) for his rigour, Madeleine Castaing (*see* pp. 132–5) for her poetry, Henri Samuel for his taste." Architecturally, he sees Frank Gehry and I. M. Pei as geniuses. In his profession, he supports those who look beyond the present: "Philippe Starck (*see* pp. 180–5) interests me – he thinks about the future and does it with a sense of humour – and Andrée Putman (*see* pp. 102–7), who also does something different, although what they do is stylistically the antithesis of what I do."

Grange continues to extend himself in many directions – although he also finds time for "ordinary" life, going skiing and swimming. He toys with the possibility of taking on film- or theatre-set design (being an ardent moviegoer, and a fan of Fellini and Visconti for the element of surprise they bring to films), and is always interested in new approaches. "For the first 20 years in my work I was constantly surprised. I am not so surprised any more – except by Anouska Hempel, whose Zen approach was a surprise; I like it but I don't do it. These days, I am not so easily impressed except by work itself. Now I make time to travel and am motivated by what I receive from that experience. I like to go to faraway places. I like Japan. I am interested in the future and what it will bring us in this field by way of new materials."

With an extensive and varied collection of artifacts spanning the past two centuries, his most precious possession is the Paris apartment in which he lives, in the elegant Palais Royal, once the home of the famed bohemian writer Colette. "I like understatement and my own epoch. I like to live in my own times, but that can mean an amalgamation of other epochs, other places and things I like to have around me."

Jenny Armit

"My life has been about serendipity. I believe in making the right thing for the right person, in that marriage of place, person and space."

Cultural crossover is a trademark of Jenny Armit's interiors, mingling British, Spanish, Sri Lankan and American influences. She combines these with an architect's sense of space and light, an astute sense of colour, extensive knowledge of 20th-century artifacts and furniture, and a sophisticated eye. Her look, developed over the years, incorporates strict modern lines with curvilinear neo-Baroque forms. Armit's work ranges from domestic projects (such as a London house for Peter and Felicity Osborne, of the fabric and wallpaper firm Osborne & Little) to US telephone company AT&T's centre at the 1996 Olympics in Atlanta, Georgia – where she transformed a 60ft (20m) interior wall by treating its surface with luminescent hologramatic gilding, with the AT&T logo subtly visible in the design.

Left: The study-cum-guest-room in a late Victorian London house decorated by Jenny Armit features padded walls and drapes in Bordeaux velvet, a cast-bronze lamp with a fabric shade by Hannah Woodhouse, a custom-made rug by Christine Van Der Hurd and a lucite version of Gerald Summer's 1930s plywood chair.

Armit's style reflects time spent in different countries. "My homes are always eclectic but the elements of eclecticism change. As life moves on, you keep some things and abandon others." Her colour sense grew from the light in sunnier climes, "but I adore the light in London too, the subtlety of tone."

Born in London, Jenny Armit grew up between Ireland and England, attended boarding school in England, and then travelled to Mexico and

India. "I love being a foreigner. It became almost a professional occupation. You have to make an effort as a foreigner, you have to absorb different manners." After meeting her husband, four years were spent going backward and forward to Sri Lanka, where she worked with Women's Rural Development on fabric projects for women who had no dowries. "It was hands-on, going into villages in an artisanal spirit – the women had the skills but didn't know how to make the results attractive to another eye."

Ireland was again home for a while, then Majorca, where she studied Spanish language and culture. The Armits bought an old palace, abandoned for 40 years, on the east coast: "a magnificent house," which Jenny restored with local builders, adding modern elements: "I really believe houses tell you what to do." Commissions followed, but she chose formal training in Madrid, studying Interior Architecture at IADE art and design institute. After being headhunted by Rosa Bernal, she started her own company in Madrid.

Three years later the family moved to Britain. "In London at that time, every man's wife was a decorator, and I decided to do something different. I found interesting designs and furniture designers through the Crafts Council. David Gill was my mentor – he was very supportive and educated me in the historical side of the 20th century." The interior of a house in Hampstead, working with architect Piers Gough, launched her career in London in the early 1990s. "Interior design is a generous profession for women because you are not judged on anything but your experience and skill. Architecture is much harder on women; there are very few top women architects – Eva Jiricna and Zaha Hadid are two in London – but there are many top women interior designers."

Armit now leads a bi-continental life: Jenny Armit Design and Decorative Art Inc is based in Los Angeles, while Jenny Armit Interiors is based in London. Her gallery on Los Angeles's Melrose Avenue (the design of the space itself is indicative of her skills) is packed with modern classics: glass sculptures by Danny Lane, sofas by Michael Young, chairs by Tom Dixon, and metalwork by Mark Brazier-Jones, alongside rugs by Christine Van Der Hurd and fabrics by Celia Birtwell – "the idea is to showcase the marvellous talent Europe has to offer under one roof on the Pacific Coast." (A Californian photographer commented, "Like David Hockney before her, it takes a Brit to teach the Californians about colour.") Armit's own furniture, including her "Homage" sofa and ripple sycamore pieces, is mixed with Gio Ponti chairs and other classics: "The intention was not to create a retro environment but show contemporary pieces in context."

Nowadays it is California that stimulates her aesthetic sense. "Staying in a Schindler house in Silver Lake, California, was a pivotal experience. Being in America has made me notice the 20th century. My attitude to architecture used to be not unlike Prince Charles's. Then I saw Chicago, which was completely exalting, something else again."

Above left: The entrance hall in the London house has black and white tiles, yet the walls are painted lavender and the Victorian chairs are covered in vivid colours. **Right:** The light-drenched drawing room with stone fireplace contains a stacked glass console by British glass sculptor Danny Lane, a 1950s armchair with fabric designed by textile artist Celia Birtwell, and a coffee table of Armit's design with two of its top squares upholstered for seating.

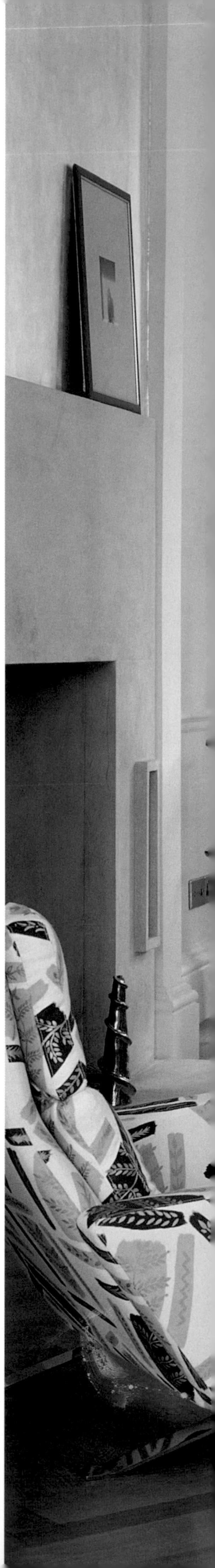

ORGANIC

The notion of "organic" covers a range of interpretations. For some, it has meant design following the natural form of living things, curvilinear and resisting mass production; this look is linked with the Arts and Crafts movement and Art Nouveau. Others, such as the architect Frank Lloyd Wright, have focused on design with a spirit in keeping with the fundamental nature and function of an object or place. These two approaches have resulted in a modern style that is moulded, often plastic, and can today be mass-produced – a form of organic both natural and unnatural.

Above: Every detail in the work of Belgian Art Nouveau architect Victor Horta was animated by scrolling stems and whiplash tendrils, seen here on a banister in Hôtel Solvay in Brussels (designed in 1895, completed in 1900).

Previous pages: In the Art Nouveau-style Hôtel Solvay, curves take precedence, structural supports are exposed metal (reducing the number of internal walls), and organic motifs and ornament are used for details such as the light fittings and door handles, giving a unity to the interior.

Interior design inspired by nature owes much to the Arts and Crafts movement and Art Nouveau style, which both peaked in popularity at the end of the 19th century. Their effect was to shift the focus of design onto craftsmanship and a comparatively simple, organic look.

The Arts and Crafts movement was influential from the mid-19th century in Europe, reaching its apex between 1888 and around 1910; in the United States, it spanned from 1875 to the 1910s. Evolving in reaction to a proliferation of poorly designed machine-made products, its aim was to promote ideals of craftsmanship in the face of industrialization. In America and Europe alike, the movement helped widen the debate about what constituted good design, but had little direct impact on interior design, partly because its exponents neither invented a style nor adhered to one in particular. They took inspiration from Gothic, neo-Georgian, *japonisme* and, eventually, Art Nouveau (the latter responsible for a prevalent organic, nature-inspired look) and incorporated these elements into designs.

Indirectly, however, the movement had great influence over perceptions of the interior: it prepared the way for the Art Nouveau style through its philosophy of design and ornamentation, and for the Modern movement through rigorous discussions of design and architecture and a simple belief that good art and design could reform society. The Arts and Crafts movement espoused the virtues of individualism and the designer's right to experiment with materials. Leading figures of the British faction of the movement included William Morris, John Ruskin and C. R. Ashbee, who, encouraged by a utopian vision, all celebrated the dignity of the artisanal craftsman and a step toward nature. Adolf Loos, Walter Gropius and other Modern-movement pioneers in Europe acknowledged a debt to the British idea of an environment that served and expressed human needs.

Through the Arts and Crafts movement, there was an impetus for a revival of national styles. Key names witnessing this process at the turn of the 20th century included the German Peter Behrens (*see* p. 96), the Austrian Josef Hoffmann (*see* p. 95), and Eliel Saarinen (*see* pp. 162–3) from Finland. Interior design had yet to emerge as a profession but, following the philosophies of the British Arts and Crafts movement, Continental architects began to approach interiors with a regard generally reserved for exterior treatments, using forms that could permeate all of a building, from architecture to interior fittings. A major triumph of the movement's protagonists was the narrowing of gaps between designer, producer, seller and consumer of goods. Arts and Crafts architect-designers focused on the object in conception and production.

Unfortunately, although mass production of goods implied lower net costs, this type of craft production proved prohibitively expensive for most people.

Art Nouveau was a decorative arts style which developed simultaneously across Europe (first coming to public awareness in Belgium) in the 1880s; it peaked around 1900 and petered out prior to World War I. The term Art Nouveau may be used in a narrow sense to denote a specific style of ornament – linear, vegetal and sinuous, with reference to the Rococo (*see* p. 11) and Auricular styles. (Auricular ornament was an early 17th-century style that evoked the curved shapes of the human ear; it was a bridge from Mannerism to Rococo, anticipating the latter's forms.) Art Nouveau was characterized by intentional exaggeration of organic forms, which took root and climbed like ivy over a basic structure; its most notable feature was a whiplash curve that gave a sense of dynamic movement. The name was taken from the Paris shop Maison de l'Art Nouveau, which opened in 1896, but the style, also called *Le Style Moderne* in France, was named differently in other countries: *Stile Liberty* in Italy (from the shop Liberty's of London), *Jugendstil* (meaning Young Style) in Germany and Scandinavia (from the Munich journal *Jugend*) and, perhaps most confusing for those following terminology closely, *Modernisme* or *Arte Moderno* in Spain.

Part of the impetus that triggered Art Nouveau was a backlash against the opulence of the Beaux-Arts and Ritz styles, which were more suited to the grandeur of a bygone era. Designers in France and Belgium made use of new materials such as iron, experimenting with the moulding and bending of pillars and beams and exploring new structural possibilities; they directed their talents toward the middle classes and intelligentsia rather than the aristocracy. Particularly in Belgium and Italy, Art Nouveau was linked with socialism – Victor Horta (1861–1947), its Belgian originator, was invited in 1896 to design the Brussels Maison des Peuples by the chief socialist party in Belgium, as his style was considered fitting for a meeting place for workers' organizations.

In Spain, Italy and Russia, Art Nouveau expressed new national and political aspirations. The city of Barcelona, capital of the Catalan region of Spain, gave birth to an Art Nouveau style in attempting to escape Spanish domination. The style's most prominent architect-designer in Barcelona was Antoni Gaudi (1852–1926). Gaudi was inspired by organic sources (including human skeletal structure), Arabian art, the French architect Eugène Emmanuel Viollet-le-Duc (who believed that structure was itself an architectural expression), the Arts and Crafts movement, and his own desire to work without historical reference. Nonetheless, traces of Catalan Gothic style are present in much of his work and the influence of Medieval art is evident in his 1900-2 crypt and transept of the

Below: Charles Rennie Mackintosh's hallway at Hill House, in Helensburgh, Scotland (1902), designed for the publisher Walter Blackie and his family, combines geometric motifs with Arts and Crafts principles. The rectilinear motifs and box-like forms indicate Mackintosh's association with the Vienna Secession and the Wiener Werkstätte. Mackintosh studied the habits of the Blackie family before embarking on the design of the house.

Above: In the living room of Frank Lloyd Wright's house, Fallingwater, at Bear Run, Pennsylvania (built in 1936), large windows help to harmonize indoors with outdoors; the walls are in "organic" rock-masonry, and the furniture in North Carolina walnut. Built on rocks, the structure (in concrete) cantilevers over a waterfall.

cathedral of La Sagrada Familia in Barcelona. Gaudi's fervent nationalism and religious belief were expressed through the individuality and emotion of many of his outrageous designs for apartment blocks, houses and churches, still considered some of the most futuristic visions of the 20th century.

Josep Maria Jujol (1879–1949), a member of the younger generation of Catalan Modernista architect-designers, an apprentice of Gaudi and often mistakenly considered a mere follower and emulator of his master, collaborated on many Gaudi projects in Barcelona, including the Casa Battlo and Casa Mila. Jujol's decorative work presaged the Surrealists and Expressionists, as well as his own architecture such as the extraordinary and curvaceous Torre de la Creu in Sant Joan Despi (1913), nicknamed the "*Casa del Ous*" or "House of Eggs."

Although Art Nouveau reached its apogee at the Paris 1900 exhibition, the International Exhibition of Decorative Art in Turin in 1902 provided the most comprehensive international overview of the style. Interiors on view included examples by Victor Horta, the Dutchman Henri van de Velde, and the French architect and designer Hector Guimard (1867–1942), best known for his rhythmical cast-iron subway-station entrances and florid ornamentation for the Paris Métro. Italian designers whose careers were promoted on a worldwide scale by the exhibition included Carlo Bugatti (1855–1940), a member of the car-designing family, whose exotic organic interiors, inspired by Africa, used unusual materials such as vellum and pewter inlay. The suite of rooms he showed at Turin included the *Camera de Bovolo*, or Snail Room, with furniture based on the snail-shell. *Stile Liberty* continued to flourish in Italy for nearly a decade after 1902, when in other European countries Art Nouveau had passed its peak.

Apart from some regional variations, two main forms of Art Nouveau emerged. In the first, French and Belgian exponents such as Guimard and Horta worked in an intricate and fastidious manner. The second was a more rectilinear and ordered style, developed by the Scottish architect Charles Rennie Mackintosh and seen in the work of members of the Vienna Secession (*see* pp. 94–6), and eventually carried through to the Deutscher Werkbund (*see* p. 96), where, in more simplified form, it was applied to industrial design.

Technological advances in manipulation and bending of materials into organic curves had great impact in shaping interior spaces. In 1964–8, Eero Aarnio's bulbous space-age "Pastille," "Tomato" and "Bubble" chairs in fibreglass resin exemplified a renewed passion for the rounded form in furniture. The success of organic design has been aided by the development of plastics, and in the 1980s by computer-controlled wood-cutting and -shaping and an increase in the use of moulded aluminium, due to a drop in its raw-material price.

Organic Functionalism

In America, New York's Museum of Modern Art launched a competition and exhibition in 1940–1 called "Organic Design for Home Furnishings" with an aim to highlight furnishings of an organic nature. Charles Eames (1907–78, *see* pp. 166–7) and Eero Saarinen (1910–61, *see* pp. 163–4), widely considered the two most prominent American postwar designers, jointly won prizes in the competition, having interpreted the theme by showing moulded plywood chairs, "organic" in that they expressed the wave or curvilinearity of natural forms. Since then, organic design has come to be defined very loosely as any form demonstrating curvilinearity: a biomorphic form imitating the appearance of living things.

This interpretation of organic as biomorphic is something of a deviation from its original meaning, whose foundations lie in the concept of organic architecture, developed by the American architect Frank Lloyd Wright (1867–1959) under the influence of the teachings of architect Louis Sullivan (1856–1924). In his *Kindergarten Chats* essays of 1896, Sullivan published the dictum: "Form ever follows function. This is the law." He claimed, "It is really the essence of every problem that it contains and suggests the solution." Form, therefore, can exist in the design task itself, and need not necessarily be based on traditional aesthetic values. This could almost be interpreted as Functionalism, a term revealing a way of design-thinking rather than representing a particular style. The word Functionalism was also used by the Modern movement (*see* pp. 92–123), although there it became interchangeable with Rationalism (meaning making the best of available materials).

In the case of Functionalism within organic parameters, the end product may not appear organic or even curved. The organic nature of the design is the result of the form and function being one and the same; in its purest meaning, organic is taken to mean "having a complete organized unity," "fundamental to the nature of a thing."

From this standpoint, Frank Lloyd Wright developed the teachings of Sullivan and his own methods and philosophies. He argued that a building should have its own identity and, being part of

Above: At Saarinen House, Cranbrook Academy, Bloomfield Hills, Michigan, the dining room, with its view through to the living room, has a table and chairs designed by Eliel Saarinen in 1929 and made by The Company of Master Craftsmen in 1930. The rug, hanging lamp, firemantle, peacock andirons and *torchères* were all designed by Saarinen, while the upholstery and wall hanging are by his wife Loja. The dining centrepiece bird is by Franz Hagenauer.

a landscape, should also express its relationship to its immediate environment and be in harmony with nature in its use of materials and colour.

Having learned the foundations of architectural design and theory in the Chicago offices of Dankmar Adler and Louis Sullivan, Wright went on to establish a distinctive American style for both domestic and commercial interiors. Working at the start of the 20th century, he shared the concern of his European counterparts for integrated interiors, believing that an interior should provide a flowing and unified space, sympathetic to the entire building and its surroundings. His "Prairie" houses proclaimed not only his architectural genius but also his lifelong involvement in all things that defined a living space: furniture, lamps, rugs, fabrics, even ashtrays. The Organic School, as Wright called it, began in the United States with suburban lifestyle and an appreciation of American home-grown architecture. He branded this style "Usonian," from "United States own."

Wright and his European counterparts also shared a dislike for historical precedent. Architects and designers on both sides of the Atlantic were seeking to create a truly new vision. Ludwig Mies van der Rohe, describing the effect of a Wright exhibition in Berlin in 1910, wrote: "The encounter was ... to prove of great significance to the European development. The work ... presented an architectural world of unexpected force, clarity of language, and disconcerting richness of form."

Cranbrook Academy of Art

In the years before the First World War – when architects such as Mackintosh in Scotland, Voysey in England, Wright in the American Midwest and the Greene brothers in California were participating in the development of the "organic" interior by making furniture part of its surrounding spaces – Eliel Saarinen (1893–1950), an early Modernist, was following the Arts and Crafts tradition of his native Finland. In 1923, Saarinen won the $20,000 second prize in a competition for the design of the Chicago Tribune Tower in the United States (first prize went to Frank Lloyd Wright). A passionate traveller, he used the money to emigrate to the United States, where he joined the staff of the University of Michigan before becoming involved in the Cranbrook Academy of Art, 20 miles from Detroit in Bloomfield Hills, Michigan.

The academy was founded in 1925 by George C. Booth, a Canadian-born newspaper publisher who nurtured the idea of a utopian arts community based on both an American ideal and reinvigoration of the Arts and Crafts idea. It comprised an education community of four learning institutions and a church. Saarinen's first commission was to design the Cranbrook School for Boys; this was such a success that in 1926 he was invited to work on the Cranbrook Academy of Art. The Kingswood School for Girls followed in 1929, a project in which the entire Saarinen family participated.

Eliel Saarinen became the leading creative force behind the academy, and was resident architect from 1925 until 1950 and academy president for 1932–6. The first generation of faculty and students comprised mainly Europeans, including Saarinen's family: his wife, Loja; daughter, Pipsan; and son, Eero (probably best known for his 1962 curvaceous interior of the TWA terminal at JFK International airport in New York). Among the second generation were Midwesterners Charles Eames and Florence Knoll (*see* p. 164). In 1936, Eliel Saarinen introduced scholarships in painting, architecture and sculpture, which increased attendance in the years that followed. Other graduates of the academy included silverware designer and sculptor Harry Bertoia, sculptor Carl Milles and textile designer Jack Lenor Larsen.

At Cranbrook Academy, the building now called Saarinen House was originally the home and studio Eliel Saarinen designed for himself and his family, aided by family members and artists and artisans from the academy. His wife, who headed the academy's Department of Weaving in 1929–42, designed the textiles and played a significant role in the garden design; Eliel himself was responsible for the architectural form and much of the furniture. Thought to be the most thoroughly conceived and integrated work of art, architecture and design in the United States, the house – completed in 1930 – has been described as one of the most significant houses to be built in 1920s America, a total work of art. Today it is restored to its former condition, after painstaking research and liaison with its one-time inhabitant, Roy Slade, fifth president of Cranbrook Academy. It is now a museum, with the original furniture returned, including the handsome dining table and chairs made from holly wood inlaid with ebony.

Saarinen's influence on aesthetics in the 20th century goes beyond his achievements at the academy. His "formula" for architecture was described by writer Claude Bragdon in his 1932 essays as "simple, rectilinear masses, the verticals rising sheer without dissenting lines." This particularly pertains to Saarinen's designs for high-rise buildings, which exerted a profound influence on American skyscraper design during the boom of the 1920s.

Later generations of Cranbrook-trained designers are said to have been inspired by organic, amoeboid forms and a Modern but humanistic aesthetic, and to have regarded mass production positively as bringing "good design" to the mass market. Their approach echoed that of architect Charles Greene (1868–1957 – together with his brother, Henry, he built "California Bungalow" houses in the early 1900s, and was known for a

Below: In the living room and studio at Saarinen House, the smoking table is designed by Eliel Saarinen and made by Tor Berglund (1931). The hanging lamp with spun and coppered shade is also by Saarinen, as are the "Kingswood" auditorium armchairs in tubular chromed steel, wood and woven upholstery (1929–31). The rugs are by Loja Saarinen (the larger "Exhibition" rug is an original). "Head of a Dancing Girl" is sculpted by Carl Milles (1917).

Above: The classic "Tulip" dining table and chairs were designed in 1956 by Eero Saarinen, son of Eliel and Loja, and manufactured by Knoll. The base and seat were visually incorporated to form a sculptural continuum through inclusion of a central stem (and by base and seat being the same colour), although the pedestal base is aluminium and the seat fibreglass.

meticulous, lyrical style); when the public turned away from his architecture in the 1920s, Greene retaliated: "Artists don't have a chance. The educated people want skill, not soul." Two decades later, Cranbrook designers realized that the public wanted technology, and only the most brilliant architects and designers could also supply "soul." From the 1940s, they produced furniture that challenged European dominance and combined the production-line methods with sensitive design.

The first chair to be mass-produced in plastic was Charles Eames's "Shell" chair (1949), with its single moulded unit for seat and back. Eero Saarinen described a chair as a "three-dimensional object always seen within a room, which is essentially a box," and posed the question, "How do you relate this object to the box? The Cubists, the De Stijl designers, Ludwig Mies van der Rohe and Le Corbusier all saw this fundamental relationship and solved it by their light steel furniture – truly beautiful thinking and truly beautiful furniture. Somehow technology has shifted. New materials and techniques have given us great opportunities with structural shells of plywood, plastic and metal." Furniture and interior spaces were changing.

The Knoll Furniture Company, founded in 1938 and run from 1955 by Florence Knoll, mass-produced such pieces. She also established the Knoll Planning Unit for interior design in 1946, creating contract interiors based on the Mies aesthetic (*see* p. 98) of simple, geometric but expensive finishes. The firm still manufactures Mies's 1948 "Barcelona" chair for placing in Mies interiors, with other design classics of the 20th century, including Bertoia's wire-mesh diamond chair. The other prominent furniture manufacturer of the time was Herman Miller Inc, which mass-produced leading examples of Modern furniture designed by sculptors, such as a 1944 palette-shaped glass-topped table by the organic sculptor and designer Isamu Noguchi (1904–88, active in the United States and Japan).

Postwar European design

Throughout the postwar era, American furniture design reached Europe by way of magazines such as *Domus* (*see* p. 101). In Italy, the government was attempting to encourage, with US funding, a national spirit based upon liberal democracy. Since the strict lines of the Modern movement were associated with prewar Fascism, curvilinear, organic inspiration proved a welcome alternative.

Italian design played a substantial role in the creation of the Post-Modern "organic" interior. During the 1950s and early '60s, Italian furniture was arguably the most voracious and adventurous in the world. The Museum of Modern Art in New York held an exhibition in 1972 entitled "Italy: the New Domestic Landscape," which showed specially commissioned micro-environments by the leading radical designers Ettore Sottsass (born in 1917, *see* pp. 172–7), Mario Bellini (born in 1935) and Joe Colombo (1930–71, *see* pp. 178–9), challenging ideas on the home environment and Modernism. Sottsass and Colombo, inspired by space travel, designed modules that could be rearranged for flexibility. For Colombo, a designer was a "creator of the environment of the future," to which end he produced designs to provide an "integral habitat." However, the 1970s in Italy were a time of political turbulence and terrorism: modern furniture production came to a virtual halt, and Italian designs seemed to lack their usual energy.

In France, official encouragement of Post-Modern design has contributed greatly to the renaissance of interior design since the 1980s. The then President of the Republic, François Mitterrand, was in the vanguard when it came to promoting design, and commissioned several young designers to decorate the private apartments of the Elysée Palace in Paris in 1983. Among these new talents was Philippe Starck (*see* pp. 180–5).

In the mid-1980s, the Israeli designer Ron Arad (born in 1951; designer of Israel's New Tel Aviv Opera House foyer) produced monumental biomorphic sheet-metal sculptural furniture from his British-based company, One Off. Individuality and idiosyncrasy are the essence of Arad's approach – an echo from the early 20th century.

Most recently, in 1998, the British designer Roger Dean's "Home for Life" project showed a fresh and futuristic approach to the organic home: a curved, womb-like house structured around plaster casts taken from fibreglass moulds, sprayed with concrete, and strengthened with steel rods (exteriors are tiled or grassed over). Dean explains, "My aim is to reverse the Bauhaus philosophy of houses being machines for living. Instead, houses should respond to human, emotional needs, in particular the desire for comfort and security."

Art Nouveau, generally considered the precursor of the biomorphism witnessed in design for homes in the 20th century, has had an enormous impact on how we see interior space. The fluidity of "natural" form has found its place during the past few decades, softening some harsher elements of contemporary design. From public buildings to a simple vase, the curvaceous line is omnipresent. Today the creations of Charles Eames and Eero Saarinen sit alongside those of Philippe Starck. As recently as 1991, the Design Museum in London held an exhibition entitled "Organic Design," and magazines such as *Wallpaper** in the late 1990s continued to promote innovation in organic design.

Below: One of the most prominent works to date by London-based Israeli designer Ron Arad (in collaboration with Alison Brooks of Arad Associates) is the New Tel Aviv Opera House foyer, designed in 1988. Light bounces off the bronze curves of its sweeping amphitheatre staircase, amplifying the biomorphism of the design.

Charles and Ray Eames

In 1985, seven years after his death, American designer Charles Eames (1907–78) was voted the world's most influential designer by the prestigious body the World Design Conference. His wife and partner, Ray (1912–88), should perhaps have shared the accolade, since in their 40 years together her contribution to his work was immense, and he often insisted that she was "equally responsible."

Full of ideas and enthusiasm, the Eameses epitomized the American Dream shared by many in the mid-20th century, and had the drive and energy to realize it. After the rough years of the Depression, they believed in progress, and in the optimism of postwar America anything seemed possible. The couple's exuberant creations embraced consumerism, yet incorporated elements of playfulness, glamour and enjoyment of beauty in everyday objects. Their ideas left a lasting legacy in the design world, thanks to the vitality of their furnishing designs, their participation in advancing technology for furniture, and their endless experimentation; many top practitioners today award the Eameses pride of place in their hearts.

Charles Eames was not only a designer but also an architect, scientist, craftsman, inventor, teacher, film-maker and photographer. Having studied architecture at Washington University in St Louis, Missouri, he worked for an architectural firm before setting up alone. From 1938 to 1940, he was Head of Experimental Design at Cranbrook Academy (*see* pp. 162–4), and worked with Eero Saarinen (*see* pp. 163–4) investigating the artistic possibilities of new materials that allowed greater organic expression.

It was at Cranbrook that Charles met Ray. She was studying weaving, ceramics and metalwork (after training as a painter), and showed an acute sense of colour, composition and structure in her early graphics and sculpture that anticipated the couple's later collaborations. They married in 1941 – Ray's wedding ring was designed by Harry Bertoia.

In 1940–1, Eames and Saarinen won awards for their moulded plywood chairs at the "Organic Design in Home Furnishings" competition in New York, and an entirely new look for furniture was born. Eames and Saarinen were also among the first designers to understand that open-plan interior architecture focused furniture away from walls, so that it had to be seen as free-standing sculpture, and space around it dealt with differently.

Manufacturers were reluctant to take up the moulded designs, since production costs for the compound curves were prohibitive, but the Eameses were not to be thwarted. Moving to Los Angeles, where Charles took a job designing film sets, they worked at night to find a way to bend plywood in more than one direction. From their experiments came a contraption with a bicycle-pump attachment and an inflatable membrane.

Continuing experiments during the war, the couple developed light, durable moulded plywood splints for the US Navy, and set up their own company, later merging with Evans Products Company. Through their experiments, it became possible to make quality bent-plywood furniture inexpensively and in volume. Other technological strides followed in aluminium and plastic, and the Eameses' plastic moulded "Shell" armchair of 1949 became common in homes, cafés and schools the world over.

The Eameses' own home in Pacific Palisades, California, is unusual and endearing. A box-like house built in 1949 from off-the-shelf machine-made components, the exterior is rectilinear and strict, the inside brimming with the couple's own furniture, American folk art, plants and antique toys.

Many Eames pieces are produced again today. They include the "Shell" chair, the black-leather "Chair and Ottoman" of 1956 (which Charles said should have the "warm, receptive look of a well-used first baseman's mitt") and "*La Chaise*," from a 1948 prototype. Eames furniture is widely used by other top designers to complement their work.

BIOGRAPHY

1907	Charles Eames born, St Louis, Missouri.
1912	Ray Kaiser born, Sacramento, California.
1920	Charles took up photography.
1933	Ray began studying at Art Students League, New York, under avant-gardist Hans Hofmann.
1934–8	Charles set up Eames & Walsh architects, St Louis.
1938	Charles took up fellowship at Cranbrook Academy.
1940	Charles won joint first prize with Eero Saarinen at MOMA.
1941	Ray and Charles married, and moved to Los Angeles.
1941–2	Charles worked in art department at MGM.
1945–9	Charles and Ray designed house for John Entenza (editor of *Arts & Architecture* magazine) and their own house at Pacific Palisades.
1949	Designed "Shell" chair.
1956	Designed "Chair and Ottoman."
1978	Charles died.
1988	Ray died.
1997–8	Comprehensive exhibition of their work worldwide.

Left: Charles and Ray Eames built their prefabricated house in 1949 in Pacific Palisades, Santa Monica, California. Its open-plan interior, arranged by Ray, housed chair designs by Charles (here, a 1956 lounge chair and ottoman made from three moulded rosewood shells with leather upholstery and cast-aluminium base), as well as paintings and textiles by Ray and the couple's curious collection of American folk art.

Michael Taylor

"In the final analysis, new ideas are simply solutions to new problems.... My creed is simplicity, and I think this is always the most sensible approach.... If a room is kept simple, and if it works well, nine times out of ten it looks well."

Michael Taylor (1927–86, born in Santa Rosa, California) worked mainly in San Francisco, where he developed a much-copied naturalistic style of interiors and furniture that was initially a blend of southwestern US and Mediterranean influences. His "California look" brought nationwide publicity to America's West Coast. Beige-on-beige or white-on-white, incorporating natural stone (he was particularly fond of Yosemite slate and fossilized stone), the style had signature elements of logs, wicker and wood in a near-natural state, and was accented by mirrors, plants and spherical cushions in plain and acid colours – the latter derived from ancient China.

First inspired by a boyhood introduction at a neighbour's home to the innovations of Elsie de Wolfe (*see* p. 62), Taylor consistently denounced the cluttered, the sombre and the pretentious. He disliked overuse of trinkets and lived by the somewhat prosaic expression, "when in doubt, throw it out." His early interiors, choice of neutral colour palette and desire for simplicity were influenced by Syrie Maugham (*see* p. 63), who helped create the "white look" popular in the United States of the 1920s. "At that time white in all shades was

Left: This ocean-front house on La Chuza Point, in Malibu, California, was designed by Taylor and built in 1983 by architect John Lautner (who trained under Frank Lloyd Wright). It features river-bed boulders that break up the geometry of the architecture, and slabs of slate as free-form floor covering. The dining chairs are in Greek Klismos style.

frequently used almost to the exclusion of other colours in certain fashionable houses, but in the intervening three decades, with the rapid and almost frenzied prewar and postwar succession of fads, gimmicks, trends and trick schemes, white was almost forgotten," Taylor wrote in his 1960s essay 'A New Look at Decorating,' published in the book *The Finest Decorators*. Another influence was the American decorator Frances Elkins. Taylor acquired most of Elkins's business estate when she died, including items bought from Maugham.

It was Taylor's originality in creating a new look during the late 1950s – a look that was appropriate for the West Coast climate, combining indigenous materials with articles from other cultures – that gave him a place in history as a designer. Taylor explained, "The climate of my native state, the quality of light, and the ready availability of plants and of various types of growing things all contributed to bringing about what has been hailed by many as a new look in decorating. The underlying quality of this new look can best be described as rooms in which a feeling of air and lightness predominates.... This type of decorating may be easier in California than in many areas where the climate is more inclement."

A vital factor for Taylor was the "problem of light" – how much natural light is available in a room by day and how it is illuminated by night. He liked the "feeling" created by white lamps "because of the bright way colours react to them," and his designs placed great importance on the effects of differing exposure to light in a room, "all of which is part of the theory and mechanics of light." He found he could use proportionately very little colour, yet achieve an effect of colour and brightness. When questioned about his use of "non-colour," he said, "There is a tremendous amount of colour in my rooms, but there are not many colours. Light, as we know, contains in itself all colours, so that from the simple background the main colour I use in the room travels rapidly and with no competing wavelengths to the eye."

With a passion too vigorous for the tiny and the precious, he mixed elements from disparate origins: "If a room is too rich, or if the furniture is all too ornate, or all too primitive, the room is wrong. It is contrast that brings it excitingly alive." He used calico and rough silks alongside bleached woods, and grouped objects from locations as diverse as Morocco, Tokyo, Mexico and Majorca.

In San Francisco, Taylor studied at the Rudolf Schaeffer School of Interior Design. After a partnership with Frances Milhailoff, from 1951, he set up his own practice in 1956. In 1960, he opened a shop on Sutter Street, San Francisco. According to Dorothea Walker, a friend of Taylor's and magazine editor (she worked for American *House Beautiful* and under Diana Vreeland on American *Vogue*), he had acquired a huge quantity of hexagonal white tiles and wanted to create a shop space using them. Also according to Walker, his choice of location was superb: the shop neighboured the Elizabeth Arden beauty salon where California's finest flocked in droves. Once coiffed and manicured, customers passed by almost as part of their beauty ritual, giving Taylor a captive audience for his displays.

At least 30 of Taylor's projects were photographed in the 1960s, '70s and '80s for *Architectural Digest*, *House & Garden* and *House Beautiful* by top photographers such as Horst, including Norton Simon and Jennifer Jones's Malibu house, architect John Lautner's Malibu house and Jimmy Wilson's Arizona villa; 17 made the magazines' covers. Taylor's light, natural style soon became a cornerstone of modern organic design.

Right: The simple living area in the La Chuza Point house, built on a rocky promontory, comprises built-in seating as well as oversized "Log and Rush" chairs by Michael Taylor, along with spherical cushions of his design that are inspired by findings from the East. The house has naturalistic slate floors throughout. Large, leafy plants are also a signature of Taylor's interior schemes.

Ettore Sottsass

"There is no doubt that, sooner or later, something will be done so that one can put on one's own house every day as we don our clothes, as we choose a road along which to walk every day, as we choose a book to read, or a theatre to go to."

Born in 1917, the Italian designer Ettore Sottsass is perhaps best known for his distinctive Post-Modern furniture – in particular that designed in conjunction with colleagues in his Memphis group. An architecture graduate from Turin Polytechnic, Sottsass served in the Italian army during World War II. Afterwards, in 1946, he set up a studio in Milan and began designing furniture and interiors for postwar housing, as well as ceramics, scarves and book jackets. At home, he also worked on abstract sculptural projects. At the Milan Triennale design expo in 1948, he exhibited designs combining rectilinear Rationalism with organic shapes. Work in the George Nelson studio in New York in 1956 was followed by a return to Milan and a post, in 1958, as design consultant to Olivetti's electronics division, where he redesigned the company's first computer. On further trips to the United States in the 1960s, he encountered Pop Art and pop culture. During the 1970s, Sottsass divided his time equally between Italy and Spain, living in Milan and Barcelona. In 1972 he contributed to New York Museum of Modern Art's "Italy: the New Domestic Landscape," where he showed an interior of movable linking units.

Left: Sottsass transformed Max Palevsky's beach house in Malibu, California. In the living room, Sottsass's furniture is as dominant as the art by Frank Stella (on the left) and Roy Lichtenstein, whose 1968 wall relief, entitled "Palevsky Explosion," hangs over the fireplace. The blue-glass-domed canopy with spiral columns reflects Sottsass's love for India.

In 1979 Sottsass joined Studio Alchimia, formed in Milan in 1976 by Alessandro Mendini, successor to Gio Ponti (*see* p. 101) as editor of the magazine *Domus*. When the new Sottsass style hit Milan later that year, it was revolutionary, not intellectually or ideologically but in spirit. Moving away from the repetitiveness and minimalism of International Style, Sottsass worked with a small circle of colleagues to resurrect everything orthodox Modernism had turned from: incongruous combinations of fine and funky materials; flamboyant shapes; bright colours; brash patterns; and – probably most controversial – hand-crafted, blatant luxury. In 1981, Sottsass left Studio Alchimia and set up his Memphis group (a name inspired by the Bob Dylan song "Stuck Inside of Mobile with the Memphis Blues Again").

The group created a sensation, and outraged serious architects and designers. More interested in audience response than in method of crafting, Sottsass flouted the notions of taste bound up with Modernism. Furniture was faced with brightly patterned plastic laminate, and inspiration was taken from mass culture, making everyday objects into design icons. The message was clear: applied art could be industrialized as an intrinsic part of design.

The Memphis group had enormous impact on interior design following their show-stopping introduction at the 1981 Milan Furniture Fair. That same year, Sottsass opened a Memphis shop in Milan, displaying his designs alongside those of other Post-Modernists. The French decorator Andrée Putman (*see* pp. 102–7) advised fashion designer Karl Lagerfeld to buy Memphis furniture and paint his walls gray to allow it to dominate. Thanks to Putman's passion for Memphis, the Paris office of France's Minister of Culture had a facelift with a Post-Modern slant in 1985. In 1987 and 1991, the Blum Helman gallery in New York held exhibitions of Sottsass's work and, in the late 1980s, some remarkable pieces commissioned by Blum Helman and produced under Sottsass's supervision outside the Memphis group were priced as high as $30,000.

Although Memphis began with furniture, it also influenced interior design – particularly in the United States. Developments in American art meant that a bolder, brasher look with unusual proportions became acceptable. Visually, Memphis design worked in tandem with paintings by popular artists of the era, and today pieces by Roy Lichtenstein and Frank Stella sit well with Memphis room dividers (as in art collector Max Palevsky's house in Malibu, California). In Europe and Japan as well as North America, the style paved the way for a new look for interiors of commercial establishments, from hairdressing salons to fast-food chains, emulating the colourful surface effects that are a signature of Italian Post-Modern design.

Sottsass continues to diversify. He completed his first architectural project, in Colorado, aged 73.

Above left: In the home of Max Palevsky and his wife Jody Evans, a pair of Sottsass tables entitled "They Thought It Was Coming From Burma" are positioned beneath "Persane" by Matisse and "*Le Repas Frugal*" by Picasso. **Right:** In the same house, a red-lacquer cabinet by Sottsass, typical of the strength of his design as it moved away from the spindly furniture of his Italian predecessors, stands in a room leading to the garden.

The photograph (*right*) shows a modest 1997 Sottsass-designed kitchen in a house in Maui, Hawaii, with simple, practical coloured elements. With the Memphis group, Sottsass wanted to create "freshness and happiness with colour." He had learned, he said, from the works of Picasso that only three colours should be visible from any vantage point. Suggestions for re-creating the crispness of the kitchen are shown in the sample board.

Wall decor

The walls have been painted in ochre-based tints. Pantone swatches **(1)** were used to specify paint colours and paints were mixed to match.

Surfaces

Coloured laminates **(2)** – here from Abet Laminate – were used for cupboard surfaces, for ease and efficiency of cleaning and durability. The work surfaces (prep-top) and stove-surround are stainless steel **(3)**, wrapping around underneath the frame for easy maintenance and simplicity of form, as well as bringing the colour spectrum to a more muted level.

Tiles

The splashback behind the sink is mustard tile from Daltile **(4)**.

Flooring

The floor **(5)** is in ash, but could be created in light oak or teak.

Equipment

The stools are from Global Industrial Equipment, the ceramics by Ettore Sottsass for Bitosi, and the kettle by Aldo Rossi for Alessi. The lamps are "Classics" by Halophane and the pulls on cupboards "Custom" by Details.

Design signatures

Ettore Sottsass's designs represent a series of thought-provoking ideas, rather than simply a series of products ready to put on the market. In this kitchen, Sottsass considers "all the elements that have been invented, to supply as efficiently as possible the traditional catalogue of needs our industrial-productive society has drawn up." There is the stove on which to cook, the refrigerator to keep food in and work surfaces for its preparation, a lamp to see by, and stools for seating, but nothing more. It is a kitchen for people who don't feel a need to flaunt their status, or to be surrounded by memories. But despite this highly pragmatic approach, there is a great deal of liveliness and *joie de vivre* in Sottsass's work.

Humour

Rejecting the utilitarian, even minimalist, restraint that has often been imposed by Modernism, Sottsass introduces frequent touches of humour and vibrance to enliven the living environment in his designs.

Colour and pattern

The antidote to cool neutrals, Sottsass's furniture and other domestic products brought both strong colour and vibrant patterns back into the modern interior.

Practicality

Sottsass's work is organic in that it focuses predominantly on shaping designs so that they are appropriate to their function. He approaches furniture as a group of movable boxes, containing functional elements for living, which can be linked together, separated, and relinked in a different arrangement, as required. His aim is to encourage a down-to-earth attitude to material objects, and avoid venerating their value or fragility.

Joe Colombo

"I don't think of myself as an artist nor as a technician, but as an epistemologist.... A designer is the creator of the environment of the future."

Milanese Joe Colombo (1930–71, born Cesare Colombo) was an organic designer in that he believed in creating an "integral habitat," where the look of a home grew out of the way it was to be used as an environment for living. Principally an avant-garde painter and sculptor, he studied painting at Brera Academy of Fine Arts, then architecture at Milan Polytechnic. In 1954, when northern Italy was promoting itself as a model of young urban consumerism, he exhibited open-air areas, with televisions (then uncommon in Europe) as focal points, at the Milan Triennale expo. This both anticipated the role of television in 20th-century life and set the tone for his modular designs – "Rotoliving" and "Cabriolet-Bed," coordinated living machines synthesizing day and night environments, were the fruit of research into living concepts, taken from his home. The "Total Furnishing Unit," shown at New York's Museum of Modern Art in 1972, represented a futuristic habitat without dividing walls, where use of space is determined by furniture. Colombo played with lurid colour and technological and functional innovation; his forms, incorporating injection-moulded plastic, are instantly recognizable as products of the 1960s.

Left: Aiming to produce designs that provided an "integral habitat," Colombo produced his "Rotoliving" unit, here set up for dining. His 1969 "Cabriolet-Bed" can be seen in the background. Colombo approached the interior as a system made up of modular components, and favoured use of new materials and forms in mass production.

Philippe Starck

"The 21st century will not be mystical. It will be very human. Man will become an affective being. He will produce his own system of signs. We shall see a complete dissociation of functional services and the senses."

France's "bad boy" of design – an image promoted by his ruffian appearance, love of motorbikes and non-conformist attitude – has probably helped shape the perception of the modern interior, in both Western and Eastern worlds, more than any other living designer in the 1980s and 1990s. Architect, furniture designer, industrial designer, humanitarian, teacher and conceptualist, Philippe Starck has formed our toothbrushes (for Fluocaril), televisions (for Telefunken), bedside lamps (such as the popular "Miss Sissi"), café chairs (the three-legged "Café Costes" chair is a staple) and global symbols (he designed the Olympic Flame for the 1992 Olympic Games). His designs range from small items that took on iconic value in chic homes of the early 1990s – as diverse as lemon squeezers and door handles – to large interior commissions in North America such as the Delano hotel in Miami, the Royalton in New York and the Mondrian in Los Angeles.

Left: In the kitchen area of Philippe Starck's house-cum-office on the Île St Germain in Paris, chairs by Charles Eames (*"La Chaise"*, foreground) and Tom Dixon (in front of the piano) mingle with Starck's own table and chair designs for Driade. Collections of African masks in the hallway and blue pitted Vallauris ceramics from the 1950s add a human touch.

As he himself admits, Starck had no "cultured" foundation and very little formal education in design, but, from his youth, he admired his father's work and understood that the most important thing about design is "what it will bring to the person who will use it." His father, André Starck, was a successful aeronautical engineer: "I was born under my father's drawing board. Inventing is all I ever inherited directly from my father. Inventing is probably the only proper profession there is, since it is really about looking deep into yourself." As a child, Philippe was more interested in the mechanics of aircraft design than the aesthetics. In those days, before computer technology, success in designing aircraft relied on the ability and eye of the engineer. The biomorphic form so prevalent in the adult Starck's work can be seen to bear some relation to the curves of aircraft bodies.

Today, Starck works with pencil and paper, as did his father. He designs for "people" rather than "consumers," and often considers his children when planning new concepts. His daughter Ara and his young son Oa both offer inspiration. One of Ara's drawings even served as artwork for a stool named for her in 1985 and, more recently, in 1996, a table lamp in the form of a vase and flower in Murano glass was named after Oa.

Born in 1949, Starck grew up in and around Paris; he attended the school of Nôtre Dame de Sainte Croix in Neuilly, just west of Paris, and then for a brief spell in 1968, aged 18, studied architecture at the Nissim de Camondo school in central Paris. He spent much time hurtling around on mopeds (and now has motorbikes in every major European city, all started by the same key). Later in 1968, having experimented with inflatable furniture, he produced his first piece, the folding "Francesca Spanish Chair." Abandoning his studies, he took a position with the fashion and accessories firm Pierre Cardin in 1969, becoming artistic director of the company. In the 1970s he followed an undistinguished career as an independent designer until, in 1976–8, he achieved acclaim for his zany interior architecture of two Paris nightclubs, La Main Bleue and Les Bains Douches. In the early 1980s, along with other designers such as Jean-Michel Wilmotte (born in 1948) and Ronald Cecil Sportes (born in 1943), he came to public attention for his furniture and interior design for French President François Mitterrand's private suite at the Elysée Palace in Paris.

In 1982, the VIA (the French body *Valorisation de l'Innovation dans l'Ameublement*) awarded Starck its *Carte Blanche* for his "Miss Dorn" chair; in 1984 it sponsored him to design another chair, exhibited at the VIA gallery. When the owner of Café Costes in Paris spotted its curved back and three legs, he commissioned Starck to design Café Costes, and the designer gained superstar status overnight. Until its closure in the mid-1990s, the restaurant's interior continued to inspire young designers, and it became a focus of pilgrimage for the world's fashionable

Above: In a corner of the vast sitting room in the Paris house-cum-office, a tabletop arrangement with designs by Starck for Alessi includes a vase with flowers, entitled "*Pour la Vie*" (1990), in marble and glass. **Right:** Decorative ceramic shells with twinkling fairy lights border the room, which contains two tables by Starck for Driade; this one has a basin and disposal pipe incorporated into the design. The table can be sat at for dining or stood by for lunch on the move. Tie-backs on the chairs are a modern version of a traditional idea. The pleated fabric lampshade is also by Starck.

café set. The radical bathrooms (utterly simple, with interesting use of mirrors) were seen as a monument to contemporary design. By 1990, the "Café Costes" chair had sold 400,000 copies. Starck was appointed artistic director of the newly formed French firm XO, creating the 1984 furniture range for 3 Suisses, the company's mail-order home-furnishings operation. Later he produced a "kit" house for 3 Suisses (a box of plans and instructions for a wooden open-plan house, available by mail order), the result something between a Thai pagoda and a Canadian mountain house.

His first domestic project (architecture and interior) was the house of a friend, Bruno Le Moult, on the Île St Germain, near St Cloud on the outskirts of Paris. This slim, gray, concrete townhouse, completed in 1987, is 18ft (5.6m) wide by 230ft (70m) long and epitomizes the simplicity of house design in the late 1980s and early '90s, with its glass and metal furniture, interior cement details and neat lamps and accessories. The Le Moult house is now neighboured by one of Starck's own houses – a mint-green, metal-slatted townhouse with a warm but spartan wood-panelled interior; completed in 1996, it doubles as his Paris office.

By 1987, Starck's work had been shown in 30 exhibitions in the United States, Japan and Europe; 1988 saw his ground-breaking display of French design at the Pompidou Centre in Paris, later mounted in London on a more modest scale. This exhibition promoted Starck to standard-bearer for the French design community.

Architectural work was to follow. Buildings included the Nani Nani café in Tokyo (1989), houses and the Teatriz restaurant in Madrid (1990), and the headquarters of the Asahi Beer Company in Tokyo (1990) – the latter topped with a vast, organic root-like form, giving it a sculptural presence. More recent projects include houses in Japan, the Groningen Museum in Holland (1994), the Peninsula restaurant in Hong Kong (1994) and the Asia de Cuba Restaurant in New York (1997). He is now working on a hotel in Bali and projects for the Canary Riverside development in London.

Starck believes in looking to the future. He has taught at the Domus Academy in Milan and the Ecole des Arts Décoratifs in Paris, and received coveted awards – including three in the United States (for the New York Royalton and Paramount hotels and a Harvard Excellence in Design award in 1997), as well as being decorated *Officier des Arts et des Lettres* by the French President. Yet his outward theatricality is underlain by humility about his achievements: "My only reality and destiny is to bring about happiness." He feels that the time for designing chairs and lamps is over, and his real work is yet to come. He is particularly interested in the house of the future, which he thinks "will be reduced to an empty envelope: the temperature will be controlled from the floor, the light will be an electro-luminescence provided by windows of liquid crystals, sound and pictures will come from the walls. This will be."

Left: Philippe Starck's interior designs for hotels include the Royalton hotel in New York (1988), where the lobby displays clear biomorphism. **Above:** The lobby of the Delano hotel, Miami Beach, Florida (1995) has an exaggerated ottoman and a checkerboard of wall lights.

DIRECTORY

Abet Laminates
70 Roding Road
London Industrial Park
London E6 4LS, England
Tel: 0171 473 6910
and
100 Hollister Road
New Jersey 07608, USA
Tel: (201) 541 0701

Jenny Armit Design and Decorative Art Inc.
8210 Melrose Avenue
Los Angeles
California 90046, USA
Tel: (323) 782 9173

Avena Carpets
Bankfield Mill
Haley Hill, Halifax
West Yorkshire HXE 6ED, England
Tel: 01422 330261

Bennison Fabrics
16 Holbein Place,
London SW1W 8PL, England
Tel: 0171 730 8076
and
76 Greene St.
New York
NY 10012, USA
Tel: (212) 941 1212

Brunschwig & Fils
10 The Chambers
Chelsea Harbour Design Centre
London SW10 OXF, England
Tel: 0171 351 5797
and
979 Third Avenue
New York, NY 10022-1234, USA
Tel: (212) 838 7878

Mario Buatta
120 East 80th Street
New York, NY 10021, USA
Tel: (212) 988 6811

Nina Campbell
9 Walton Street
London SW3 2JD, England
Tel: 0171 225 1011
and
90 Commerce Road
Stamford
Connecticut 06902, USA
Tel: (203) 359 1500

Madeleine Castaing (gallery)
21 rue Bonaparte
Paris 75006, France
Tel: 01 43 54 91 71

Colefax and Fowler
39 Brook Street
London W1Y 2JE, England
Tel: 0171 493 2231
and
Cowton & Tout
979 Third Avenue
New York, NY 10022, USA
Tel: (212) 753 4488

David Collins Architecture and Design
6 and 7 Chelsea Wharf
Lots Road
London SW10 OQJ, England
Tel: 0171 349 5900

Dorothy Draper & Company, Inc.
60 East 56th Street
New York
NY 10022, USA
Tel: (212) 758 2810

Farrow & Ball
Uddens Trading Estate
Wimborne
Dorset BH21 7NL, England
Tel: 01202 876141

Flos Lighting
McInnes Cook (distributors)
31 Lisson Grove
London NW1 6UV, England
Tel: 0171 258 0600

Jacques Garcia
212 rue de Rivoli
75001 Paris, France
Tel: 01 42 97 48 70

Galerie Yves Gastou
12 rue Bonaparte
75006 Paris, France
Tel: 01 53 73 00 10

David Gill
60 Fulham Road
London SW3 6HH, England
Tel: 0171 589 5946

Jacques Grange
118 rue Faubourg St Honore
75008 Paris, France
Tel: 01 47 42 47 34

H A Percheron
G6 Chelsea Harbour Design Centre
London SW10 OXE, England
Tel: 0171 349 1590

Nicholas Haslam (shop)
12 Holbein Place
London SW1W 8NL, England
Tel: 0171 730 8623

Christine Van Der Hurd
2/17 Chelsea Harbour Design Centre
London SW10 OXE, England
Tel: 0171 351 6332
and
102 Wooster Street
New York, NY 10012, USA
Tel: (212) 343 9070

Jim Thompson (at Mary Fox Linton Ltd)
1/8 Chelsea Harbour Design Centre
London SW10 OXE, England
Tel: 0171 351 9908
and
2100 Faulkner Road
Atlanta
Georgia 30324, USA
Tel: (404) 325 5004

John Oliver
33 Pembridge Road
London W11 3HG, England
Tel: 0171 221 6466

David Kleinberg Design Associates
330 East 59th Street
New York
NY 10022, USA
Tel: (212) 754 9500

Lee Jofa
Suite 204 The Chambers
Chelsea Harbour Design Centre
London SW10 OXE
England
Tel: 0171 351 7760
and
225 Central Avenue South
Bethpage, New York
USA
Tel: (516) 842 9116

Christian Liaigre
61 rue Varenne
75007 Paris
France
Tel: 01 47 53 78 76
and
42 rue de Bac
75007 Paris, France
Tel: 01 53 63 33 66

McMillen Inc
155 East 56th Street
New York
NY 10022, USA
Tel: (212) 753 6377

Peter Marino + Associates
150 East 58th Street
New York
NY 10011-3698, USA
Tel: (212) 752 5444

Frédéric Méchiche (gallery)
4 rue de Thorigny
Paris 75003, France
Tel: 01 42 78 78 28

Nessen
420 Railroad Way
PO Box 187
Mamaroneck
NY 19543, USA
Tel: (914) 698 7799

Nuline
5-317 Westbourne Park Road
London W11 1EF, England
Tel: 0171 727 7748

Oriel Hardwood
66 Camberwell Road
London SE5 OEG, England
Tel: 0171 703 5009

Osborne & Little
304-308 Kings Road
London SW3 5UH, England
Tel: 0171 352 1456
and
90 Commerce Road
Stamford
Connecticut 06902
USA
Tel: (203) 359 1500

Pierre Frey
253 Fulham Road
London SW3 6HY, England
Tel: 0171 376 5599

Alberto Pinto
61 Quay d'Orsay
75007 Paris, France
Tel: 01 45 51 03 33

Pongees
28-30 Hoxton Square
London N1 6NN, England
Tel: 0171 739 9130

Parish-Hadley Associates
41 East 57th Street
New York, NY 10021, USA
Tel: (212) 888 7979

Andrée Putman sarl
83 avenue Denfert-Rochereau
75014 Paris, France
Tel: 01 55 42 88 55

Ron Arad Associates
62 Chalk Farm Road
London NW1 8AN, England
Tel: 0171 284 4963

Jonathan Reed/Reed Design
151A Sydney Street
London SW3 6NT, England
Tel: 0171 565 0066

Stephen Ryan (shop)
7 Clarendon Cross
London W11 4AP, England
Tel: 0171 243 0864

John Saladino
Saladino Group
200 Lexington Avenue
New York
NY 10016, USA
Tel: (212) 684 6805

Sills Huniford Associates
30 East 67th Street
New York
NY 10021, USA
Tel: (212) 988 1636

Shelton Mindel & Associates
216 West 18th Street
New York, NY 10011, USA
Tel: (212) 243 3939

John Stefanidis
7 Chelsea Manor Street
London SW3 3TW, England
Tel: 0171 351 7511

Tindle
162 Wandsworth Bridge Road
London SW6 2UQ, England
Tel: 0171 384 1485

V'Soske Joyce UK Ltd
Unit 16 The Coda Centre
189 Munster Road
London SW6 6AW, England
Tel: 0171 386 7200

Watts of Westminster
2/9 Chelsea Harbour Design Centre
London SW10 OXE, England
Tel: 0171 376 4486
and
41 West 25th Street
10th Floor, New York
NY 10010, USA
Tel: (212) 647 0303

Wemyss Houlés
40 Newman Street
London W1P 3EA, England
Tel: 0171 255 3305

Wendy Cushing Trimmings
G7 Chelsea Harbour Design Centre
London SW10 OXE, England
Tel: 0171 351 5796

PLACES OF INTEREST

Le Corbusier/Villa Savoye
82 rue de Villers
78300 Poissy, France
Tel: 01 39 65 01 06

Dorothy Draper/The Green Brier
300 West Main Street
White Sulphur Springs
West Virginia 24986, USA
Tel: (304) 536 1110

Charles and Ray Eames/Eames House & Studio
203 Chautauqua Boulevard
Pacific Palisades
California 90272, USA
Tel: (310) 396 5991

Jacques Garcia/Hotel Côstes
239 rue St. Honoré
75001 Paris, France
Tel: 01 42 44 50 25

Christian Liaigre/Hotel Montalembert
3 rue de Montalembert
75007 Paris, France
Tel: 01 45 49 68 00

Parsons School of Design
66 Fifth Avenue
New York, NY 10011, USA
Tel: (212) 229 8900

Gio Ponti/Hotel Parco dei Principi
Via Rota 1, Sorrento,
Italy
Tel: 081 878 2101

Andrée Putman/Morgans
237 Madison Avenue
New York
NY 10016, USA
Tel: (212) 686 0300

Saarinen/Cranbrook Academy of Art
1221 North Woodward,
Bloomfield Hills,
Michigan 48304-2824, USA
Tel: (248) 645 3300

Philippe Starck/Delano
1685 Collins Avenue
Miami Beach,
Florida 33139
USA
Tel: (305) 672 2000

Frank Lloyd Wright/Fallingwater
PO Box R Mill Run
Pennsylvania 15464
USA
Tel: (724) 329 8501

BIBLIOGRAPHY

Adam, Peter, *Eileen Gray: Architect/Designer*, Thames and Hudson (1987)

Ambasz, Emilio (ed.), *Italy: The New Domestic Landscape*, Museum of Modern Art (1972)

Arwas, Victor, *Art Deco*, Abrams (1980)

Baldwin William W., *Billy Baldwin Decorates*, Chartwell Books (1972)

Baldwin William W., *Billy Baldwin Remembers*, Harcourt Brace Jovanovich (1974)

Battersby, Martin, (Philippe Garner ed.), *The Decorative Thirties*, Whitney Library of Design (1988)

Beaton, Cecil, *The Glass of Fashion*, Cassell (1954)

Becker, Robert, *Nancy Lancaster: Her Life, Her World, Her Art*, Alfred A. Knopf (1996)

Brown, Erica, *Sixty Years of Interior Design: The World of McMillen*, The Viking Press (1982)

Brunhammer, Yvonne, *André Arbus: Architecture-Décorateur des Années 40*, Norma Editions (1996)

Byars, Mel, *The Design Encyclopaedia*, Laurence King Publishing (1994)

Calloway, Stephen, *Twentieth Century Decoration*, Weidenfeld & Nicolson/Rizzoli (1988)

Campbell, Nina, *Nina Campbell on Decorating*, Conran Octopus (& Clarkson Potter) (1996)

Campbell, Nina and Caroline Seebohm, *Elsie de Wolfe: A Decorative Life*, Crown (1992)

Craig, Theresa, *Edith Wharton, A House Full of Rooms*, Monacelli Press (1996)

Delorme, Jean-Claude, *Maisons d'Exception*, Editions de la Martinière (1994)

Diamonstein, Barbarelee, *Interior Design*, Rizzoli (1982)

Esten, John and Rose Bennett Gilbert, *Manhattan Style*, Little Brown (1990)

Foulk, Raymond, *Emile Jacques Ruhlmann Centenary 1897-1979*, The Foulk Lewis Collection (1997)

Foulk, Raymond and Jenny Lewis, *Betty Joel – Celtic Spirit from the Orient*, The Foulk Lewis Collection (1997)

Gombrich, E.H, *The Story of Art*, Phaidon (1978)

Gossel, Peter and Gabriele Leuthauser, *L'Architecture du XXe Siècle*, Benedikt Taschen (1991)

Hampton, Mark, *The Legendary Decorators of the Twentieth Century*, Doubleday (1992)

Hecker, Stefan and Christian F. Müller, *Eileen Gray: Obras y Proyectos*, Gustavo Gili, Barcelona (1993)

Hicks, David, *David Hicks on Living – With Taste*, Leslie Frewin Publishers (1968)

Hicks, David, *David Hicks on Decoration – With Fabrics*, Britwell Books (1971)

Jackson, Lesley, *Contemporary Architecture and Interiors of the 1950s*, Phaidon Press (1994)

Jones, Chester, *Colefax and Fowler: The Best in English Interior Decoration*, Barrie & Jenkins (1989)

Jervis, Simon, *The Penguin Dictionary of Design and Designers*, Penguin (1984)

Julier, Guy, *Encyclopaedia of 20th Century Design*, Thames and Hudson (1993)

Kirkham, Pat, *Charles and Ray Eames: Designers of the 20th century*, MIT Press (1998)

Kornfeld, Albert, *Interior Decorating and Encyclopaedia of Styles*, Doubleday & Co (1965)

Mongiardino, Renzo, *Roomscapes: The Decorative Architecture of Renzo Mongiardino*, Rizzoli (1993)

La Pietra, Ugo, *Gio Ponti*, Rizzoi (1995)

Llinas, Jose, Jordi Sarra, *Josep Maria Jujol*, Benedikt Taschen (1994)

Lovatt-Smith, Lisa, *Intérieurs Parisiens*, Benedikt Taschen (1994)

Mackay, Robert B, Anthony Baker and Carol A. Traynor (eds.), *Long Island Country Houses and their Architects*, W.W, Norton & Co. (1997)

Massey, Anne, *Interior Design of the 20th Century*, Thames and Hudson (1990)

Miller, Judith and Martin, *Victorian Style*, Mitchell Beazley (1993)

Page, Marian, *Furniture Designed by Architects*, Whitney Library of Design, (1983)

Parish, Sister, Albert Hadley and Christopher Petkanas, *Parish-Hadley: Sixty Years of American Design*, Little, Brown (1995)

Pinto, Alberto, *Alberto Pinto*, Michel Aveline (1992)

Sanchez, Diego, *Jean-Michel Frank, Adolphe Chanaux*, Editions du Regard (1997)

Sembrach, Klaus Jürgen, *L'Art Nouveau*, Benedikt Taschen (1991)

Sparke, Penny, *A Century of Design*, Mitchell Beazley (& Baron's Educational Series, Inc) (1998)

Starck, Philippe, *Starck*, Benedikt Taschen (1996)

Stephanidis, John, *Living by Design*, Weidenfeld & Nicolson (1997)

Sudjic, Deyan, *Ron Arad, Restless Furniture*, Rizzoli (1989)

Tasma-Anargyros, Sophie, *Andrée Putman*, Laurence King Publishing (1993)

Tweed, Katharine (ed.), *The Finest Rooms by America's Great Decorators*, Viking Press (1964)

Wharton, Edith, and Ogden Codman, *The Decoration of Houses*, W.W. Norton & Co (1997)

Wittkopp, Gregory (ed.), *Saarinen House and Garden*, Harry N. Abrams (1995)

QUOTATIONS

Diamonstein, Barbarelee, *Interior Design*, Rizzoli (1982) – for permission to quote: John Saladino, Mark Hampton, Mario Buatta (earlier quotes - from taped lectures at Parsons School, New York).

Tweed, Katharine (ed), *The Finest Rooms By America's Great Decorators*, Viking (1964) – for permission to quote: Mrs Henry Parish, Rose Cumming, Michael Taylor (from autobiographical essays).

INDEX

Page numbers in *italics* refer to illustrations.

Witt, Count and Countess de 17
Wolfe, Elsie de *see* de Wolfe, Elsie
Wood, Ruby Ross 30, 59, 131
Wright, Frank Lloyd 61, 95, 157, 161, 162

ACKNOWLEDGMENTS

With special thanks to: Albert Hadley

Also to: Jenny Armit, Trudi Ballard, Jean-Pascal Billaud, Mario Buatta, Nina Campbell, Antoine Castaing, Madeleine Deschamps, Jonathan Emus, Nicole Fallon, Philippe Garner, Jacques Garcia, Yves and Francoise Gastou, Jacques Grange, David Hicks, James Huniford, Tom and Yvonne Huthert, Clive Kandel, David Kleinberg, Christian Liaigre, Virginie Liaigre, Laure Lombardini, Peter Marino, Frédéric Méchiche, Lee Mindel, Michael Moran, Lesley and Adrian Olabuenaga, Brigitte Ory, Raymond Paynter, Alberto Pinto, Nancy Porter, Andrée Putman, Jonathan Reed, Stephen Ryan, John Saladino, Jane Seamon, Peter Shelton, Betty Sherrill, Ettore Sottsass, Stephen Sills, Philippe Starck, John Stephanidis, Dorothea Walker. Thank you also to the manufacturers who loaned items for the "design signature" photo shoot: Abet Laminates, Avena Carpets, Colefax and Fowler, John Oliver, Lelièvre, Nuline, Pongees, Wemyss Houlès, Wendy Cushing Trimmings.

Thank you to Min Hogg and Susan Crew for permission to quote.

And to Judith More, Janis Utton, Julia North, Claire Gouldstone and Cathy Rubinstein for their group effort.

Agence Top/Roland Beaufre 132-133, 133, 134 left, 134-135/**Pascal Chevallier** 116-117 **AKG, London** 95/**Erich Lessing** 94; **Ron Arad Associates/G. Dagon** 165 **Arcaid/Earl Carter/Belle** 114-115/**Richard Einzig** 164; **Archivio Gio Ponti** 97, 101; **Rogi André** 65 top; **Mario Buatta** 45 top; **Nina Campbell** 51 top, 52/**James Mortimer** 50-51 left, 52-53, 54-55, 55 top; **Prunella Clough** 100 right; **Colefax and Fowler** 31, 34-35, 35 top, 36 left; **David Collins/Henry Bourne** 61; **Studio Joe Colombo, Milano** 176-177, 177 top; **Conde Nast/Oberto Gili** 108-109, 110 left, 110-111 right; **Corbis UK Ltd/UPI/** 130 left; **Rose Cumming Inc.** 128 right; **Billy Cunningham** 59 **Madame Figaro/Giacomo Bretzel** 109 right/**Vincent Knapp** 147 **Decoration Jacques Garcia/Marie Clairin** 15/**Marianne Haas** 14-15/**Jaussin** 12, 16-17, 18 **Philippe Garner** 64 right, 65 bottom, 126, 127/**Berenice Abbot** 100; **Yves Gastou** 69 right; **The Greenbrier Hotel** 130 right; **Guy Hervais** 13, 19 top; **Evelyn Hofer** 92-93, 96, 156-157, 158, 172-173, 174 left, 174-175; **Hulton Getty Picture Collection** 137; **The Interior Archive/Fritz von der Schulenburg** 124-125, 136-137, 138, 138-139, 140 left, 140-141 right, 142-143, 143, 144 top left, 144 top centre, 144-145 top right, 146-147, 148-149, 150 top left, 150-151/**Christopher Simon Sykes** 28, 29, 30, 112-113 top/**Edina van der Wyck** 4-5, 152-153, 154 top left, 154-155; **Jean Francois Jaussaud** 66-67; **Nadine Johnson/Michael Mundy** 116; **Melba Levick** 1, 168-169, 170-171; **Christian Liaigre/Serena Laudisa** 115 right; **Mc Millen Interior Design and Decoration** 33 bottom; **Frédéric Méchiche** 67; **Derry Moore** 26-27, 36-37 right, 44-45, 46 left, 46-47, 48-49, 56-57, 62 right; **Michael Moran** 2, 118, 120-121, 121, 122 top left, 122-123 top right; **Michael Mundy** 72-73, 74-75 left; **Parish-Hadley** 41 right, 74 left, 76 left, 76-77 right/**Debranne Cingari** 73 right/**Oberto Gili** 42-43 right/**K. Haavisto** 42 left/**Wilbur Pippin** 33 top, 128 left, 129, 131, 169 top/**Keith Scott Morton** 40-41 left **Alberto Pinto** 21 top/**Brigitte Baert** 98, 99/**Giorgio Baroni** 6-7, 8-9, 20-21, 24-25 /**Roland Beaufre** 10, 11, 22 left, 22-23/**Jacques Dirand** 25 **Octopus Publishing Group Ltd/ Tim Clinch** 58, 68-69, 70 left, 70-71 right, 180-181, 181, 182, 183/ **James Merrell** 38-39 centre, 82-83/ **Neil Mersh** 18, 38-39, 86-87, 112-113, 140-141, 176-177 top/ **Kim Sayer** 159; **Undine Pröhl** 176-177 centre; **Andrée Putman** 103; **Reed Creative Services/Adam Beaumont-Brown** 89/**Ken Hayden** 88-89, 90 top left, 90 top centre, 90-91 top right; **Paul Rocheleau** 160, 162, 163; **Stephen M.P. Ryan/ Henry Wilson** 60; **Paul Ryan** 78-79, 80 left, 80-81; **John Saladino** 79; **Deidi Von Schaewen** 102-103, 104, 104-105, 106-107, 107 top right; **Julius Shulman** 167; **Sills and Huniford** 83, 86 bottom, 86-87 top/ **Thibault Jeanson** 84, 84-85; **Sotheby's London/Cecil Beaton** 32, 62 left, 63; **Ettore Sottsass/Luca Bianchi** 173; **Philippe Starck** 184, 185 **Roger-Viollet** 64 left; **Mark Williams** 119.